Adventures in Parenting:

A Support Guide for Parents

Adventures in Parenting:

A Support Guide for Parents

by

Rachel C. Ross, MS Ed.

DEDICATION

I dedicate this book with love and gratitude to my mother, Doreen M. Ross, who taught me many valuable lessons, both good and challenging, over the years. I was able to heal many of my own childhood wounds through healing my relationship with her, and together our lives changed for the better.

– R.C.R.

Printed with support from the Waldorf Curriculum Fund

Published by:
The Association of Waldorf Schools
of North America
Publications Office
65–2 Fern Hill Road
Ghent, NY 12075

Title: *Adventures in Parenting*
    A Support Guide for Parents
Author: Rachel C. Ross, MS Ed.
Editor: David Mitchell
Copy Editor and Proofreader: Ann Erwin
Photos: Wendy Baker, and others
Cover: Hallie Wootan
© 2008 by AWSNA
ISBN # 978-1-888365-76-4

TABLE OF CONTENTS

INTRODUCTION

The hardest job in the world is being a good parent, and yet it is a job that comes with no training. Alas, children are not born with "how to" booklets attached to their ankles. Parenting is also an opportunity for adults to heal their own childhood by learning from their own children. Unfortunately, it also offers us an opportunity to repeat with our own children the mistakes of our parents. If we do not learn from the past, then we are destined to repeat it. One of the biggest burdens for parents is feeling guilty for their shortcomings, mistakes and inadequacies. These feelings are often based not on the reality, but on what the individual perceives he or she has or has not done. The feeling of guilt can be passed down through generations as a maternal or paternal legacy.

Becoming a parent is a thrilling and often scary prospect. Most parents share with each other their dreams and fears for their children. They feel they could do more for their children, but are ill-prepared. They are surprised at how different their children are from each other: "My first child was so easy, calm, happy, not demanding. But my second child hit the deck running. He seems to be learning everything at a rapid pace, and we are having difficulty keeping up with him." This scenario has also been stated in the reverse: the first child was the challenging one, while the second child is more calm and even able to help the older sibling. The point is: Each child is unique, although all children progress through archetypal stages of human development.

The major factors to be examined include on one side, the essence of the individual child: Who is the actual person revealed in the child in front of us? and on the other side, the child's karma (destiny), the imprints of heredity and environment upon the make-up of that child. Thus we see that understanding each human being and his or her life is not a simple task. Many of the reasons we are who we are can be traced back to past-life experiences imprinted into the karma of this lifetime.

> *What I see is just the covering.*
> *The most important is invisible.*[1]
> —A. de Saint Exupéry (1900–1944)

PARENTING STYLES

My father gave my build to me,
Toward life my solemn bearing,
From mother, comes my gaiety,
My joy in story-telling.
— Johann Wolfgang von Goethe (1749–1832)

"Parenting style" refers to the quality and gesture of how a person parents. We look at it in a manner similar to how educators observe learning styles to help them be better teachers in the classroom. When we are able to view our style of parenting objectively, we have the opportunity to observe what is good and what needs to be changed for the well-being of our children and our entire family. To understand how we parent, we must delve into our own nature and remember how we were parented. Are we repeating the past? This process can be both challenging and uncomfortable, but it is nevertheless essential in order to develop ourselves to become healthy, successful parents.

Psychologists have set up a category format of three to four parenting styles to help describe particular types of parents. It is important to keep in mind that whenever we narrow human behavior down to specific diagnostic terms, there is the danger of over-simplifying and/or labeling at the expense of the whole picture. This happens frequently in the diagnosis of children as well. Once the diagnosis and labeling is complete, a further tendency arises for all subsequent investigation and observation to cease. Even the question as to why the person displays these behaviors is often lost. But to truly change the way we parent, we must look back into our own childhood and into our own emotional/mental makeup to understand why we behave in a particular manner. What are we getting out of this process? What is the effect upon the children who are the benefactors or victims of our behavior?

Since at least the 1920s, developmental psychologists have been interested in how parents influence the development of their children's social and instrumental competence. One of the most robust approaches to this area is the study of what has been called "parenting style." This Digest defines parenting style, explores four types, and discusses the consequences of the different styles for children. Parenting style captures two important elements of parenting: parental responsiveness and demandingness.[2]

—Maccoby & Martin

Parenting Styles Based on the Four Temperaments

There are many different ways to view parenting styles. One way is from the point of view of the four temperaments and the effects of each on children.

Temperament stands in the middle between what we bring with us as individuals and what originates from the line of heredity.[3]

— Rudolf Steiner

The ancient Greek philosopher and father of modern medicine, Hippocrates, viewed the human body as having a balance between four humors: blood, phlegm, black bile and yellow bile. A person became ill due to an imbalance in his humors, and a treatment was designed to return the humors to a balanced state. The four humors formed the basis for medical treatment well into the Middle Ages.

1. ***Blood*** was related to a person with a lively personality and high energy. This type of person enjoyed life and the arts.
2. ***Phlegm*** caused a person to be lethargic or dull.
3. ***Black bile*** caused depression and sadness.
4. ***Yellow bile*** caused anger and a fiery personality.

This is a very basic, simplistic view of personality types. Human beings are more complicated and diverse than just these four elements. Rudolf Steiner addressed the nature of the human being from the point of view of four temperaments in a lecture entitled *The Mystery of Human Temperaments* (1908):

The fact that the temperament is revealed on the one side as something that inclines towards the individual, that

*makes people different, and on the other side joins them
again to groups, proves to us that the temperament must
on the one side have something to do with the innermost
essence of the human being, and on the other must belong
to universal human nature. Our temperament, then, points
in two different directions. Therefore it will be necessary,
if we wish to solve the mystery, to ask on the one hand:
How far does the temperament point to what belongs to
universal human nature? And on the other: How does it
point to the essential kernel, to the actual inner being of the
individual?* [4]

As adults we are all able to access these four temperaments
or qualities of personality, but most of us display one or two
temperaments predominantly. When this is true we are out of
balance, which can adversely affect others, especially our children.

1. **Choleric** – Blood: fiery, enthusiastic, willful, take charge
2. **Phlegmatic** – Glands: watery, unruffled, sustaining
3. **Melancholic** – Bones: earthy, sensitive, thoughtful, mull it over
4. **Sanguine** – Nerves: airy, creative/artistic, spontaneous

Applicable to parents and teachers alike, each temperament,
when too strong and out of balance with the other elements, can
have a powerful effect upon children. The adult is in the power
position. A controlling, choleric teacher can cause children to appear
melancholic. These children might have rebelled at first, but when
they are continuously "punished" for their "uncooperative behavior"
and they are either sent from the home or classroom, they become
withdrawn and appear to be melancholic (sad or depressed). The
phlegmatic parent is often a consistent nurturer but has difficulty
with discipline because discipline takes effort and confrontation.
This parent holds to routines out of comfortable habit, not in order
to control.

A melancholic parent or teacher also has an imbalanced effect
on children when every day he or she presents with gloom and
doom, a "glass half empty" attitude. No discussion will change this
perspective, which lies like a great weight or pall upon everyone.

On the other hand, an out-of-control, sanguine nature can be equally frustrating because many projects get started but nothing is completed. Like at the Mad Hatter's Tea Party, one topic is started, and before it is finished, a new one is begun. This behavior can create chaos, stress and confusion in the family and classroom. A sanguine mother is always late for everything because she is too scattered and cannot prioritize. There is no ill will in this, but it still has a negative effect upon children.

Mainfest in human beings living and working with others, these four temperaments are helpful at different times and in response to different people or circumstances, and a reasonable person will draw on them appropriately. Steiner gave indications to teachers about how to work with the temperaments of children in their care. Likewise, how parents meet the temperament of the child can either help the child come into balance or compound the negative qualities.

1. The sanguine should be able to develop love and attachment for one personality.
2. The choleric should be able to develop esteem and respect for the accomplishments of the personality.
3. The melancholic should be able to develop a heartfelt sympathy with another's destiny.
4. The phlegmatic child should be led to share in the interests of others.

This also applies to how we adults treat each other and how we work on our own temperamental configurations at a constitutional level, deeply imprinted into our entire makeup and unconscious. We all know how difficult it is to change a habit. The process of self-education and transformation is not easy, but it is essential. The indications for meeting the children have within them helpful steps to educate ourselves as adults.

In his book *Understanding Our Fellow Human Beings,* Knud Asbjorn Lund offers further explanations and suggestions for adult self-work in relation to the temperaments. Although the book has not been revised since 1965 and is somewhat dated, the general observations of the temperaments on the grid provide a helpful overview.[5]

Important Points to Consider

It is important to keep an open mind and a non-judgmental view of the temperaments. We are complex beings, multi-faceted, and dynamic individuals. Many elements have helped to mold our constitutional makeup and personality. Heredity and environmental influences must be considered. A strong constitutional tendency can be passed on from parent or even grandparent to future generations. The forceful temperament of a parent or teacher can deeply affect the presentation of a child's constitutional or temperamental make-up. What is not inherited directly through the ancestral line can be passed on through our own behavior and how we influence a child's development. We are also able to transform our temperament and constitutional makeup through discipline, training, remediation and education. Becoming conscious of our nature and its effects upon others is the first step to change. Next comes the decision to change and to take responsibility for our thoughts, feelings and actions. As we are often a combination of temperaments and not just one, we may respond in a particular way to a particular event, often dependent on repeated past experiences.

Temperaments

Choleric: Element of Fire
- Stocky in build, healthy, "can do" attitude
- High energy, take-charge type
- Often enjoys good health
- Wants to get the job done
- Self starter, does not always understand why others cannot keep up
- Strong will forces, a "go-to" type of person
- A leader
- Can be a know-it-all and a bully
- In danger of having a fiery temper

Phlegmatic: Element of Water
- Not easily ruffled
- Consistent, staying-power type
- Good at maintaining the well-being of the entire family through daily rituals and routines, nurturing through food and festivals
- Slow to act and to react
- Thorough, and once motivated, has sustaining forces
- Does not overreact to events
- Routine and rhythm of daily life is very important; not always good at cleaning up and clutter (It takes effort to throw things out!)
- Long memory
- Can become choleric when pushed or overwhelmed
- In danger of being "lazy" or not making an effort, overweight, never finishing anything, avoiding work

Melancholic: Element of Earth
- Sensitive, lack of vitality, can be sickly
- Good caregiver, has sympathy for other's pain
- Likes to discuss every aspect of a topic
- Tends to feel everything personally, difficult to forget
- "Glass half empty" negativity, often feels overwhelmed
- Problems can seem bigger than they really are.

- Thoughtful, thinks before acting
- In danger of always being negative and too self-absorbed

Sanguine: Element of Air
- Quick to react
- Spontaneous, live-in-the-moment type
- Sympathetic, sunny disposition
- Creative, sensitive
- Very social, "life of the party," often the creator of the party
- "Glass half full" positivity
- Tends to be inconsistent and disorganized
- Difficult to keep routines or be on time
- Often does not follow though
- Very sympathetic, quick to anger, quick to forget
- In danger of not finishing any project

Choleric Parenting Style

The choleric parent is the center of the family. Everything that happens is related in some way to the needs or deeds of this parent. Everyone else in the family tends to give up his/her own wishes in service to the choleric head of the household. When projects are started, everyone has to jump in and take part. Nothing is ever done on a small scale. When out of balance the choleric parent dominates through personal power; his/her agenda overrides everything else: "It's my way or the highway!" Consequences are clearly stated and followed through on with no negotiation. Often the spouse and children learn how to "manage" the moods and temper of the choleric parent, giving into his/her demands and then quietly getting on with their own agendas, while the choleric parent is so absorbed in self that this dynamic is not even perceived. However, when perceived, the choleric feels very hurt, still oblivious to what his/her own behavior has created. The choleric parent is in danger of bullying everyone in the family, becoming abusive and even physical—the tyrant instead of the revered leader.

When a choleric teacher stood behind her young
students at an outdoor May Festival, it was obvious that
her presence was strongly felt by her students. The
children were sitting quietly on the grass, well-behaved,

16

and listening to a concert of their older schoolmates. Two little boys sat close to each other, quietly pulling up little bits of grass and, with small tosses of the wrist, flipping the grass on each other's knees. They did not look at one another or make a sound. No one saw them but their teacher and me. She cleared her throat and said, "Boys!" in such a way that a shudder went right through their bodies and souls. I could see them fold in upon themselves and shut down. I said to the teacher, "Lighten up!" and she replied that their behavior was not allowed. It was not the words she had said, but the powerful impact of invalidation that went into the children. This is an example of a negative quality of this temperament, out of balance.

Phlegmatic Parenting Style

This type of parent is in the water zone, either drawing into him/herself or spreading out over everything. Easy-going, unruffled, loves comfort and food, satisfying daily needs—nothing is a big issue or problem. "Always put off today what you can easily do tomorrow" is the phlegmatic's motto. This temperament can border on laziness and passive apathy on the one side, to being steadfast, consistent and thorough on the other. The flip side of this temperament is the choleric. When a phlegmatic is pushed too hard or too fast, he/she will turn around with choleric ferocity! It is often difficult to ascertain whether a person is actively resisting action or is a true phlegmatic. Another negative trait is that of self-satisfaction. The phlegmatic makes little effort to do the necessary work in the faculty, in school, or in the family at home. A picture of a fat, over-indulged emperor sitting on a throne comes to mind. It is important to remember that in this modern, fast-paced, multitasking world, we all need to become somewhat phlegmatic for our own sakes as well as for that of our children! Patience and inner tranquility are the marks of a true phlegmatic; the tortoise wins the race through unrelenting perseverance and inner self-assurance. Who does not need more of this in their lives?

A few years ago a teacher told me about a girl in her first-grade class who was of a phlegmatic temperament. The child had a sunny, easy-going disposition and enjoyed school. The child's mother shared that, after learning how to knit, the child's favorite pastime at home was to sit in her little rocking chair knitting her scarf (which quickly became six feet long and growing!) and singing to herself about everything she was going to eat for dinner. Now this is a happy phlegmatic child!

A teacher once shared with me that a colleague of hers drove her crazy sometimes because of his phlegmatic, slow-paced, lethargic temperament: "It's like pushing a boulder uphill!" But she also said that she greatly valued this same colleague because he kept the entire faculty from making hasty decisions that were not first carefully thought through. He always took his time to fully digest every proposal before giving his opinion and/or acting upon it.

Melancholic Parenting Style

Melancholic parents tend to be too intellectual, analyzing every event. They are often cold, not affectionate, and can dampen the joyful soul of a young child. They tend to never forget or to let go of things, getting stuck in the past. The negative aspect of melancholia can be that parents turn every situation at home into an issue about them and focus all the emotional energy on their own personal needs, not on the needs of the child or the family as a whole. This is exhausting for children and can gradually make them depressed. For the child, making an effort seems insurmountable or pointless.

A colleague with melancholic tendencies talked continually about how tired she felt all the time. Every day she had a new ailment. No matter how much support or encouragement others gave her, it never seemed to shift her melancholic state of mind, which seemed to be a bottomless well that could never be filled. One day I decided to agree with my colleague; I became totally sympathetic and reflected to her the same worry and concern for her health and fatigue. This did the trick! She said, "Do you really think that things with me are that bad?" I said that it seemed so from what she was saying. She burst into laughter when she heard her own words and realized how self-indulgent and gloomy she had sounded. Shortly afterwards, we objectively discussed a solution to help her situation. She just needed to stand outside herself for once to be objective and to see clearly.

Sanguine Parenting Style
The sanguine parent is fun, creative, flamboyant, social, busy and kind. This same parent can cause chaos and confusion, can be superficial and caring but having no depth. Few promises are kept, which creates anxiety for young children who need consistency and routine. More energy is spent on people and projects out of the home than on the family. The children are often late for school and forgotten at pick-up time at the end of the day. The car or van is a mess with clothes, toys, food, and so forth, reflecting the state of both the home and the daily "routine." In the fable of the Tortoise and the Hare, guess what temperament the hare is?

When a group of adults asked a ten-year-old, "How does your mother know so much about children?" the child replied, "She doesn't know anything about us; she just reads books about us." This mother was always lecturing others on the best way to raise children, expounding on every new theory available in mainstream literature. In reality, she could not deal with or meet the needs of her own children on a daily basis.

What does a balanced parent look like? Are there any around? What are we striving to become as a parent? Here are some elements to look for…in an ideal world.

The Balanced Parent
- Takes responsibility for parenting, is the "ego" in the house and the person in charge. The "buck stops here."
- Not predominantly one temperament, not one-sided, but able to call up the traits of all the temperaments in responding appropriately to particular events
- Practices unconditional validation of children, even when disciplining them

19

- Able to create and maintain good daily and weekly routines for the whole family
- Strives to never lie to his/her children, to be truthful and honest
- Creates healthy boundaries for children and for the family through daily routines, rhythms, rituals and appropriate rules, and follows up with concrete, effective, appropriate consequences
- Looks at him/herself first instead of blaming others
- Is a good listener, even when the going gets tough
- Is nurturing and able to discipline self and children
- Is a good role model for the children and for partner, worthy of imitation
- Is willing to change for the betterment of self and others
- Spends quality time with children individually and with the family as a whole
- Sets clear and attainable expectations for self and children
- Works to maintain an honest and loving relationship with partner
- As a single parent, sets up healthy relationships with extended family and friends to support self and children
- Is able to have fun with children and to BREATHE!

Balancing the temperaments is a lifelong process and requires personal time to renew forces and keep things in perspective. Often mothers feel that they are alone in the parenting department, and the phrase, "I am dancing as fast as I can!" applies. But when parents give up their power base and let the children take over, perspective is lost and responsibility is misplaced—everyone becomes miserable, out of control and angry. The latest writings on parenting all say basically the same thing. It all comes down to the parents; when they change, so does the child and the family. This is great news! All is not lost! It may take some hard lessons and an examination of our behavior to begin the change. One friend said, "If you do not like your life, you are the only one who can change it and make it into something you want." Further, when our children see us struggle to change and really work at it, they will have more respect for us as parents; they will trust again that someone is in charge and that they are safe and can be children again.

Prayer for Little Children[6]

From my head to my feet I am the image of God.
From my heart to my hands His breath I do feel.
When I speak with my mouth I follow God's will.
When I behold God everywhere—
In mother and father, in brother and sister,
And in all dear people,
In beast and in stone, in tree and in flower—
Nothing brings fear
But love to all that is around me.

– Rudolf Steiner

PARENTING STYLES BASED ON PSYCHOLOGICAL PROFILES

All the psychological profiles outlined below are always in danger of becoming one-sided and, consequently, of having a negative impact on the children and spouse. Whenever we become out of balance or locked into just one aspect of our nature, those qualities are destined to become destructive to others. The challenge is to recognize these tendencies and then work to change our nature, to bring it into harmony and balance.

It is often a shock when we are objectively faced with our own nature. This happens when we are confronted with the negative effects of our actions on others, especially on those we love. It is essential that we do not blame others for things we should take ownership for doing. When the "Aha" moment comes and we come to full realization of what we have done, the real work can begin. This experience can be overwhelming and at the same time freeing. The following descriptions come from observation, personal experience and conventional sources.

Passive-Permissive Parent
- Too phlegmatic, passive, not engaging with children or responding to intimate needs of the children
- Feels tired all the time. Everything is too much to deal with on a daily basis. Does not follow through on anything, especially when under stress
- Does not like, and often avoids, conflict. Can appear to not care about the events going on around
- Tends to let the child run the home
- Not a disciplinarian, which can allow, even encourage, the children to be out of control, even abusive to the parent and siblings

- Often the other parent carries the full responsibility for everyone in the family. It is either someone else's responsibility or it does not really matter enough to do something about it.

This style of parenting does not originate simply from the temperament of the parent, but also stems from his or her biography. I have met many mothers and fathers who, through childhood events, a challenging relationship or a failed marriage, feel totally overwhelmed and crippled in their will. In other words, they are passive and/or permissive parents due to depression, illness, or chronic fatigue, or because their soul/spirit has been undermined or crushed. One of the children in the family often fills the caregiver/parent role. Further, there is a lack of discipline in the house, no routine, boundaries or guidance. Children respond in different ways to this type of parenting, depending on their makeup and whatever balance is brought by the spouse.

A mother told me that she felt concerned because her only child, a nine-year-old boy, was still sleeping in the "family" bed on the upstairs outdoor deck. She was still doing many things for him every day and this caused him to not respect her, to the point where he was verbally and physically abusive toward her. She was very worried and wondered what to do. I helped her realize that she already knew what to do but did not yet have the courage to face the truth and do it. She was relieved to finally say out loud, "In loving my son, I have made him too dependent upon me, and now he seems to hate me." She had not encouraged him to learn to do things on his own at the appropriate ages. Now they were both stuck in a pattern, unable to go forward, clinging to the past. In order to help their son (and themselves), the mother and father had to first look at the situation and begin to change themselves. The second step was for the father (the passive parent) to support the mother in stopping the abuse and then for the son to have his own room.

Aggressive Parent

- Everything is an issue; displays a strong reaction to everything
- Often yells or uses a loud demanding voice
- Can use physical response to events: grabbing, shaking, spanking
- Often does not see what children need. Everything is about the adult and his or her state of mind and needs.
- Does not listen. Is focused only on own agenda and needs
- Tends to bully everyone in the family
- Can be cruel, crushing the souls of spouse and children

The least attractive qualities in anyone, especially in a parent or teacher, are sarcasm, bullying and cruelty. An aggressive parent traumatizes everyone all the time. This type of adult has difficulty seeing what he/she is doing to others; it is all about self. This behavior frequently originates in early abuse or similar trauma experienced in his/her own childhood.

Children who have an aggressive parent have a particular look about them, especially their eyes, the windows of the soul. They do not walk with confidence and honesty, and they tend to treat other children, especially vulnerable ones, as they have been treated. A sarcastic child, a bully, mocking, ridiculing others or hurting him/ herself is a child who has been abused in a similar way. It is not pleasant to hear sarcasm in a five- or six-year-old. It can be a sign that an adult or an unsupervised teenager has robbed this young child of innocence by emotionally abusing him/her.

Passive-Aggressive Parent

- Smiling at your children while actually feeling angry inside
- Controlling of others through psychological manipulation or by withholding love, or using blame, criticism, humiliation or rejection. This can often be subtle and can even appear on the surface to be the opposite.

- Always giving mixed messages to children
- What is said is not what is meant.
- Working out of hidden agendas of which the other is not informed
- Inconsistent discipline, so that the child cannot anticipate parental response to the actions of child. Often children are treated differently, depending on the intent of the parent who is manipulating the outcome.
- Practicing emotional blackmail to control partner and children
- Very good at making excuses or walking out of the room when things do not go his/her way
- At first meeting this type of person can appear to be socially savvy, intelligent, easy to get along with, fun, empathetic, and so forth. But, after awhile, the true nature begins to emerge in subtle ways.

This is one of the most manipulative types of personality. This parent can be creative and intelligent, but still a controller. The home life can be described as "walking through a mine field"; one never knows where the explosives are hidden, or when one might do something to set them off! Just when one might think everything is copacetic, the rug is pulled out from underneath. Children do not do well with hidden agendas and mixed messages, which are actually forms of lying. Untruth is presented in the guise of truth. What appears on the surface is not what is happening really. It is a no-win situation and undermines the child's self-esteem. Sometimes this type of parent is unaware of the chaos he/she is creating; however, subconsciously powerful forces are afoot.

Authoritarian Parent
- Has to be right and be perfect and has similar expectations of others
- Is very organized, systematic, and restrictive
- Can create routines, but is in danger of becoming rigid, making everyone strictly adhere to the rules
- Is good at being in charge but does not always work well with others

26

Perfection in relation to human behavior is a tricky thing. We may strive for perfection, but achieving it would mean that the goal has been reached, and there is no room for error or continued development. The word "perfect" is defined as "complete in all parts, qualities, etc.; without defect; thoroughly versed, trained, skilled, etc; of the best and most complete; to finish or complete to the highest degree."[7]

Imagine the intense pressure a child or adult is under with expectations of perfection! Such standards are not reasonable or attainable and only create high stress and self-criticism. When perfection is expected of children, we are setting them up for failure and ourselves for disappointment.

The incidence of high stress levels in children in our schools is increasing. Children who have expectations of perfection place unrealistic demands on themselves. Tense in their chairs, they sit on constant high alert. Everything they do they immediately judge critically and, often, the paper is crumpled up and thrown out.

Perfection is simply putting a limit on your future.
When you have an idea of perfect in your mind, you open
the door to constantly comparing what you have now with
what you want.[8]

—John D. Eliot, PhD

Intellectual-Critical Parent

- Talks and explains everything to the child, from an early age
- Nothing is ever right or perfect.
- Tries to build self-esteem through thoughts and words instead of deeds
- Trains children early to be self-critical and critical of others

Children of this type of parent often show a tendency either to withdraw from that parent or to become a clone of that parent. They are often very pale, unhappy and sad. They can be self-critical in the extreme, commenting on every little thing they or others do. They are brought out of their imaginative world of play into an analytical

27

view of themselves and events around them. This robs them of their childhood and makes them into miniature adults. Socializing with peers becomes quite difficult, because other children do not understand why the critical child is so nasty. There are many ways to explain things to children through imaginative pictures and not in intellectual detail.

An imaginative, sweet, first grade boy consistently says, "Oh, you mean…" and then says the opposite of what the teacher or parent has just said or asked him to do. He is anxious and self-vocalizes to help him focus. His parents are separated, and this child is expected to keep many secrets on the mother's side. "Don't tell your teacher, don't tell your father…" On the father's side, this boy is getting filled with intellectual information about every subject that arises.

One day this boy entered the classroom in the morning with his mother. He said to his teacher, "Guess what the tooth fairy left for me?" The teacher asked him to tell her what the fairy had left. At that moment the mother reached around her son and covered his mouth so that he would not tell. This poor boy does not know if he is coming or going, what is right and what is wrong.

Parenting Styles[9]

Authoritarian parent
- Values obedience and respect
- Commands the child to do or to not do
- Sets clear rules
- Unbending, does not compromise or negotiate
- Is always right
- Metes out strict punishment for misbehavior
- Child learns by imitating "expert" and following strict directions

Permissive parent
- Reacts to strict parenting styles of past by doing the opposite
- This has become a more prevalent style of parenting since WWII.
- Children are encouraged to think for themselves.
- Avoids inhibitions
- Non-conformity
- Going with the flow
- Misbehavior is often ignored.
- Hands-off approach for parenting
- Children learn from consequences of their actions.

Assertive-democratic parent
- Parent establishes guidelines for children.
- Clear boundaries are set along with the reasons for them.
- Children are taught to take age-appropriate responsibility.
- Children are given practice in making choices.
- Guided to see consequences and to problem-solve
- Misbehavior is handled appropriately while validating the child.
- Teaching vs. punishment

Polarities in Parenting Styles and Their Impacts on Children

Permissive-Passive Parent (expansive)
- Accepting of child's nature and wishes
- Validates the child as is
- Encourages child-directed decision making and activities
- Not actively responsible for setting boundaries, rules and routine
- Poor discipline and follow-through
- Reasons with child, gives explanations and negotiates as a disciplinary response to unacceptable behavior
- Parent plays the role of a "friend" or equal to the child.
- Makes few demands on the child. The child is not regularly required to do daily chores.
- Avoids exercising control or power over child, letting the child be in charge
- "It's no big deal" attitude, often displays inconsistent responses to daily events

Impact on the Child
- Poor emotional regulation and mood swings
- From willful to insecure behavioral patterning
- Rebellious and defiant when will is challenged or is made accountable for behavior
- Easily gives up on challenging tasks
- Antisocial behaviors
- No sense of boundaries, rules, or routines
- Child does not develop appropriate self-monitoring behavior skills.
- There is no role model to imitate.

Authoritative Parent (balanced)
- Is validating and disciplined
- The parent is the one in charge.

- Sets and maintains fair and equitable rules that are age appropriate
- Maintains healthy, clearly stated boundaries, rules, expectations and consequences
- Secure, nurturing, loving, consistent role model to children
- The gradual passing over of age-appropriate responsibility and independence is developed over time between parent and child.
- Healthy give and take is fostered.
- Strong bond of trust is established.

Impact on the Child
- A lively, happy disposition
- Self-confidence
- Courage to tackle difficult situations and tasks
- Not a quitter
- Healthy emotional self-regulation
- Well-developed social skills
- Can follow rules and routines
- Able to ask questions
- Can self-monitor learned behavior
- Has good sense of right and wrong

Authoritarian Parent (contracted)
- Plays strictly by the rules set by society or by self
- Strict disciplinarian with punitive response to infractions of rules
- Power and control over child is absolute.
- Active input and monitoring of child's behavior and life
- Obedience to parent values are adhered to and enforced.
- No middle ground or negotiation is allowed.
- Child's will must be compliant to parent's will.
- Respect for authority, work, rules, others (adults), tradition and structures is expected and demanded.

Impact on the Child

- Anxious, withdrawn, unhappy disposition, possible depression
- Poor reaction to frustration
- Often critical of self and of others
- Does well in school, can be competitive, but can have a fear of failure
- Not likely to take part in drugs, alcohol, negative or destructive behavior
- Spirit can be crushed.

PARENT SURVEY DESCRIPTION
AND ANALYSIS

The following parent survey was conducted over a five-month period. It consisted of a one-page questionnaire designed to elicit specific information and to be easy to complete. The participating parents were all from various Waldorf schools or attended my workshops. No names were required on the forms, which hopefully made it more comfortable for the parents to answer the questions and be honest in their answers. Most parents filled out the questionnaires during the workshops; others were sent to me throughout the period of the study by individuals and friends. Attitudes varied from being pleased to share information to not being able to even think about their own childhood experiences or their parenting styles. I am grateful to all who participated in this project for their honesty and their journey of self-discovery through taking a thoughtful look at their parenting.

Thirty-two questionnaires were returned from thirty-three families covering a total of sixty-seven children ages 3.5 months to 31 years. Six were adopted children, mostly from Central America and China. The participants were almost exclusively mothers, as either the sole or primary caregiver. Consequently, this survey had a limited gender sample base, but nevertheless revealed many interesting results. The majority of the participants were from two-parent homes; eight were from single-parent families, which included a range of divorced, separated and "single-by-choice" situations. The age range for first becoming a parent was from 21 to 46 years.

The purpose of the survey was to gather information directly from a sampling of parents covering the following questions:

- Number and age of children
- Age when first became a parent
- Structure of parenting: partnered, single, adoptive, foster parent
- Feelings about becoming a parent
- Memories of childhood and influence of own parents on parenting style
- What, if any, was the best preparation for becoming a parent
- Greatest challenge faced as a parent
- What one thing parent would change in him/herself as a parent

The overall response was there was no real training for becoming a parent. It was helpful to have good role models in their own parents and to have experiences of a nurturing, happy childhood, but that was not always the case. Many parents felt that they learned how to be a parent through "on-the-job training." They sought out friends, family and community support, observed other parents in action, and read one or more of the many parent-help books on the market today. Others found the Waldorf school parent-tot, nursery and kindergarten experiences to be very enriching and helpful in raising their children.

The range of responses to becoming a parent included both excitement and at the same time fear, one emotion arising out of the other. Another common response was a sense of blessing and, at the same time, a feeling of being totally overwhelmed or unprepared inwardly for such a responsibility. No one voiced the feeling that they did not want to be a parent. They all wanted to be parents but were unsure about the future and themselves.

One mother said that she felt "unqualified to be a parent." But what qualifications are required to be a parent? How many children would be born if parents had to show that they were fully prepared and trained to become parents? One might think that the best training for parenting would be our own childhood experiences with our own parents. Unfortunately this is not always the case. For many participants in this survey, the memory of childhood was either mixed or traumatic. Some parents said they had had a great childhood, but that experience did not extend into their adolescence. It is sad to think of all of the years that we live with our parents, and the opportunity this was for negative messages to be imprinted into our souls, messages very difficult, if not impossible, to change when we are adults. So much of our self-image is founded on childhood lessons. Unfortunately, many of those lessons leave indelible scars on our self-esteem, self-image and psyche.

It is the good memories and rituals of the past that we naturally want to pass on to our children. Survey participants expressed this very challenge: They were trying to work with the good memories and experiences from childhood rather than with the negative, striving to avoid their parents' mistakes. In this world of easy access to a vast body of information, parents have many sources from which to choose. The challenge is finding the correct fit for each particular parent, child, and family. So many parents today have not been well-parented that it becomes a greater challenge to find the right way to address specific children and situations.

When asked what one thing each parent would change in his or her parenting style, responses included: acquire more patience, take more time with their children, improve their sense of humor and reduce stress. Many participants responded that they felt overwhelmed with daily life. Very few had yet to establish a balance between the needs of their children and their own needs. It is impossible to keep giving without replenishing the coffers. Illness or some other crisis will arise which gives the parent an opportunity to stop the pace, causing the individual to "hit the wall" and be thrown back onto oneself. It can become a wake-up call to bring an awareness of the situation and to realize that to change it is for the good of all.

Other challenges experienced by participants included setting healthy boundaries and disciplining their children. Many stated that they would like to reduce their own level of stress, criticism, frustration and anger because they perceived the negative effect these qualities were having upon their children. They felt guilty about their own behavior and expressed how difficult it was to change.

Conclusion

The general consensus of the parents surveyed indicated that very few of them felt prepared for parenthood. Many stated that their childhood experiences with their parents did not provide them with enough positive memories or adequate role models to create a firm foundation for parenting their children. Many participants expressed a desire to do better than their own parents had done with them, transforming bad memories and experiences into positive ones for their own children, often not an easy task. Overcoming deep-seated habits and negative inner voices of the past takes work and conscious self-development. But the rewards are great.

Participating mothers of two-parent families faced issues similar to those of single mothers. This was especially the case when the spouse did not support them in the parenting process. The feeling of being overwhelmed by the needs of their children and the family routine was strongly felt. Of the thirty-three participants, only one mother felt confident about her parenting style and talked about her own needs rather than her child's needs.

It is clear from the responses to this survey that parents of today are looking for support and constructive education to improve their parenting and meet the needs of their children. Discipline and setting healthy boundaries are challenging processes. There is so much pressure today to fill every minute with activity that many families have no time to play together, share the experiences of the day or enjoy quiet time. Mealtimes can be quite chaotic. Many parents expressed the desire to develop more patience with their children and better methods of meeting the challenging issues their children present.

PARENTING QUESTIONNAIRE

This survey is part of a parenting project to gather information about issues confronting parents today. Being a parent is the most difficult job in the world and there is no real training for the job! Are parents getting the support they need to help their children? What kind of help do parents feel they need to be a good parent?

Please take time to read and fill out this form. Please be specific and candid. This information is confidential. When you have completed the survey, send it to me at the above street or email address. Thank you for your time and participation in this important project.

1. How many children do you have, your own, adopted, or foster? _____ Please give their ages. _____

2. Are you a . . . ?   partnered parent ☐

      single parent ☐   divorced parent ☐

      sharing custody ☐   divorced parenting alone ☐

      adoptive parent ☐   foster parent ☐

      ☐ other_____

3. How old were you when you first became a parent?

4. How did you feel about becoming a parent?

5. Do you have good memories of your childhood and adolescence? How did your experience of your own parents affect your parenting style?

6. What do you feel best prepared you to become a parent?

7. What is the greatest challenge you have faced as a parent?

8. If there is one thing you would change in yourself as a parent, what would it be?

Parenting Questionnaire Summary

1. **Number of families:** 32

2. **Number of children in family:** 1–4

3. **Children:** ages 3.5 months to 31 years
   total number of children recorded – 64 and one on the way
   one given up for adoption at birth
   adopted – 6
   foster – 2
   stepchildren – 2
   biological children at home – 54

4. **Age when first became a parent:** from 20–46 years old

5. **Family profile:**   Two-parent families – 24
                         Single-parent families – 8

6. **Feelings about becoming a parent:** Excited, nervous, bewildered, overwhelmed, happy, elated, joyful, blessed, wonderful, couldn't wait, scared, incompetent, unprepared, conflicted, unqualified

7. **Memories of own childhood:**
   - No good memories of childhood
   - No one looked out for me as a teen.
   - Mom was a yeller.
   - Good and bad
   - Sexually abused
   - Mixed memories, tried to be different from my parents
   - Wonderful memories of childhood
   - Father was verbally and physically abusive.
   - Traumatic childhood, alcoholic and mental illness in parents
   - Moved too many times, chaos at home, alcohol, arguments

- Very sad, anxious, fearful, angry
- I wish I could be more like my mother.
- Difficult divorce, harshness, painful
- Dreadful experience as an adolescent, but good early childhood
- Good parents and childhood experience
- My mom was very present, but not my dad. I picked men who were good dads.
- It was terrible; I try to be everything that is opposite to my parents.
- Mostly good, some bad, I try to work with the good.
- Good memories; my parents focused on keeping the house clean.
- Extraordinary memories of childhood, secure, stable; we had no money but lots of love.
- Good memories
- I raised myself and did not have boundaries.

8. What best prepared you to be a parent?

- My loving husband helped me learn to be a good parent.
- Instinct, good role models, reading and babysitting experience
- Getting connected with my own inner child and not putting stock in mainstream ideas
- No preparation. It was a baptism by fire.
- I always felt I wasn't good enough. I learned a lot by observing others.
- Education, meditation and a wonderful partner
- We sought out family and friends to help us.
- The loving aspect of my parents
- Listening to other parents
- Being a daughter of my own mom
- Learning to be sensitive to others, especially to children
- Went through foster and adoptive parent trainings and therapy myself
- Books and studying about how to be a good parent
- Nothing could have prepared me.

- Having a mother as a good role model; studying child development and teaching
- Having a good sense of what is right and wrong. From books. I wish I had my family nearby to help.
- I don't think that I was well prepared to be a parent at all.
- Family relationships, good feelings and things from my parents, and a good partner
- Waiting to have children as older parents

9. Greatest challenge as a parent:

- I try to be patient and understanding and selfless, but it is difficult.
- Dealing with my son's dad to ensure that my son is okay when he is not with me
- Being a single, low-income parent, dealing with negative influences of my children's dad
- Burying a child who was murdered
- My children thinking I love the other one more, and dealing with the frequent conflict between my children
- Dealing with daughter's lying, stealing and anger
- Managing the discipline of my oldest child in her teenage years
- My own demons and feelings of inadequacy or fear of making mistakes
- Not always feeling confident, instilling sense of security for my child
- Dealing with daily life and trying to meet everyone's needs
- Having the pressure to earn money while being a single parent to four children
- Not allowing my childhood issues to burden my child and wishing I had more energy and time
- Trusting myself, forgiving my mistakes, understanding my child
- Moderating society's dominating values of materialism and television influence
- Parenting a special-needs son and dealing with how society responds to him

- Balancing work and family time. We work at home and find it difficult.
- Getting enough sleep and having the energy to keep up with an active child
- Taming, accepting the hurt, angry and neglected child within me
- My oldest daughter's learning disability; moderating my expectations
- Trying not to get angry with them. With my third child it is easier.
- Feeling helpless when you know you should not do something and you do it anyway.
- Constant motion eveywhere, noise and lack of sleep are issues for me; my dislike about myself and putting it on my child.

10. What would you change in your parenting?
- Play with my children more. It is difficult to learn to do if you never did it as a child yourself.
- I need to work on developing patience, to think before speaking and not overdo it with my five-year-old.
- I feel my children's pain. I wish I could guide my children and not try to fix them.
- I am telling them I don't trust them and I need to stop doing this.
- I need more patience when I am so tired and to become a loving, better listener.
- I wish I could be more confident in myself as a parent.
- Listen to parent help tapes
- Argue less openly with my spouse and become a better example for my children
- Try to have more fun with my children
- Be less susceptible to stress and anxiety, enjoy being a parent
- Resolve the conflict between what I love to do and what my child needs, and the housework
- Have more of a sense of humor

- Not be critical of myself so that my daughter will not do the same
- Parent with sensitivity, be more patient and get more education
- Throw away the television and be firmer about enforcing my values vs. society's
- Spend more time with my husband as our children become more independent
- Patience, listening more, be a better mediator with my children
- Be kinder and lighter in voice when speaking to my child
- My high anxiety level, taking things personally, and not reacting in anger and panic
- More humor with my children
- More patience with the older children
- More patience, softness and humor; not be harsh like my mom and grandma

Healing the Past

The Impact of Our Own Parents

Over the many years I have been a teacher and therapist I have met many parents who, in sorting out how to help their children, realize that they have to acknowledge and work through their own childhood experiences. Often this involves revisiting childhood traumas that have never been confronted or healed. Many psychologists and educators say, "The apple does not fall far from the tree." This can apply to the transference of habits, ideas, trauma, feelings, attitudes and behavior to our children. In addition to their own issues, children are frequently required to carry their parents' "baggage" as well, and sometimes even the grandparents'. If we do not learn from the past, we are destined to repeat it.

A single-parent mother of two small children shared,
"My mother was a yeller. I have to work hard every day
to not become a yeller, too. It [yelling] creates stress and
unhappiness for everyone in the house and does not make
things better. I know it is up to me to change the patterns I
learned from my mother."

The Buck Stops Here:
What Are We Passing on to Our Children?

What are you passing onto your children? I am sure that it is both positive and negative. After all, we are human beings, we are not perfect, and we are in a lifetime process of figuring things out. The mistakes we make can be turned into learning tools to change ourselves and benefit our children. As a child, I watched adults saying hurtful and untrue things and saw how they affected the recipients.

Put-downs, negative criticism and "underhanded" compliments are all meant to hurt and control others. If we were criticized as a child and it damaged our self-esteem, why would we want to do the same to our own children? If our parents yelled at us all the time, and that is the unpleasant way we learned to communicate, why would we want to do the same thing to our children? It is possible to learn from negative experiences, but it takes hard work and self-development to change and heal those wounds we have carried for so long.

Parents are only human and have plenty of problems of their own. And most children can deal with an occasional outburst of anger as long as they have plenty of love and understanding to counter it.[10]

What messages that were given to us as children are we passing along our children? The things we say may not be the real messages. Children need to hear the truth, not look into our eyes and see that we mean something else. To what are children supposed to respond? To what you are saying or to the hidden agenda that they might perceive underlining what you say? Either way, the child will lose as the parent shifts the rules to fit his/her need and not the child's. When does the wheel of heredity and environment stop crushing us and do real choices begin?

A five year-old looked up into the eyes of her mother and said, "Mommy, you are smiling on the outside, but inside you are angry."

Children can perceive the truth about us at an early age. That is why so many children today are traumatized; having to carry the emotional baggage of their parents drains their own childhood away before they have the chance to truly bathe in it fully. So many children today are anxious, nervous, and angry; they throw temper tantrums and are sickly when they should be happy and healthy. Where does this come from and what can we as parents do to change the quality of childhood?

At parent pick-up time for the kindergarten, the teacher overheard one six-year-old girl say to another, "Your mother probably forgot to pick you up because she doesn't really love you." How does such a young child learn such words and concepts? Did she overhear an adult say this, or had she experienced it herself?

Being chronically late to pick up children sends them a message that the parents do not care enough to make them a priority in their lives and that the parents do not love them enough to remember them. By failing to keep a commitment or promise, the adult is not telling the truth.

In searching for healthy ways to help our children we have an excellent opportunity to help ourselves and to heal our own "inner child." We all have one, whether we acknowledge it or not. Behind every action lies a motive, whether conscious or unconscious; but the effects of the action are all the same.

A working mother of two little girls complained about her first grader saying, "She is so different from me. She whines a lot, especially at dinnertime. She hangs on me and demands food and attention while I am trying to cook. My youngest daughter is more like me and we get along better."

I asked her, "When do you eat dinner?" She told me that she picks up her daughters from their grandmother at 5:30pm on her way home from work, and makes dinner as soon as they get home. They eat at 7:00 or 7:30pm. Young children need to eat earlier and often; they need nourishment to keep their sense of life healthy. When I asked the mother if their grandmother could cook the children a full meal at 4:00 or 4:30pm each day, she said that the grandmother would love to! "But then we won't have dinner together as a family when we get home." I said that yes, you can, the children can get ready for bed and have dinner again. They just may not eat as much, but wait and see.

At this point the mother burst into tears and said, "I need the same thing as my daughter!" I pointed out that they were very much alike after all. When she looked at the real needs of her daughter, what stood behind her daughter's outer behavior, she realized she would be meeting the child's real needs and her own at the same time, a very doable situation with a win-win outcome for everyone.

It is difficult to stop reacting to or spinning along with daily life. Take time to look at your actions and the effects they have upon others. Being in denial is a destructive defense mechanism which we develop early in life for protection and to avoid responsibility for our own actions. But to truly change ourselves we must work to resolve our own feelings and stop laying blame on others.

I have come to the frightening conclusion that I am the
    decisive element.
It is my personal approach that creates the climate.
It is my daily mood that makes the weather.
I possess tremendous power to make life miserable or joyous.
I can be a tool of torture or an instrument of inspiration.
I can humiliate or humor, hurt or heal. In all situations,
It is my response that decides whether a crisis is escalated
Or deescalated, and a person is humanized or dehumanized.
If we treat people as they are, we make them worse.
If we treat people as they ought to be,
We help them become what they are capable of becoming.[11]
                                                    —Goethe

Recognizing Established Patterns

How do we recognize established patterns of behavior in our thoughts, feelings and actions? The wheel of necessity of daily life must come to a standstill each day for us to observe the effects of our behavior upon others. To begin with, all that is required is five minutes a day, five minutes a day to be still. Imagine that! But what does this mean? This can be the hardest five minutes one can spend in a day. Steiner outlined this exercise[12] as a way to begin to learn how to control one's own nature, to put the reins back into the hands of the driver. For those who are driving the wild horses of human nature, this can be very difficult. But it is essential and vital.

The Five-Minute Centering Meditation is most effective when done at the same time every day. This helps one remember to do it and builds a healthy habit of doing something positive for oneself every day. But it is better to do the exercise every day, regardless of the exact time, rather than skip a day.

- Find a quiet place to sit down comfortably, upright with feet on the floor. Do not lie down, as there is a danger of falling asleep. Turn off all phones, computer, television and radio, and so forth.
- No interruptions for FIVE minutes! For mothers it is good to do this exercise at the beginning of naptime for baby, before the children come home or, when at work, at lunch time when one can find a place to sit quietly.
- Quiet random thoughts, feelings or worries. Strive to come to complete inner quiet and stillness. This is very difficult to do because human beings are awash with a tsunami of impulses. Thoughts and feelings overwhelm us every minute of the day.
- Sometimes I imagine that I am sitting in a sphere of calm water. Slowly an emerald green light filters down through the water and through my whole body. It moves through each part of me, releasing tension and relaxing. I give up all of my stress and tension. Once the light passes through my feet into the earth, I focus on one thought or, better, a word or image, so that my whole consciousness is filled with it. I strive to hold this state of being for a few minute. After five minutes I open my eyes, breathe deeply and take another moment to get myself ready to resume the day.
- With daily practice the quiet time will become longer, and one will begin to gain more control over and a

49

healthy detachment from other areas in one's life, have more confidence and feel more centered. This is a great help for children, too. They will feel the change and will respond differently. You will have more forces with which to deal with daily life.

- Good luck. Don't give up. This process takes daily practice. Self-knowledge and change require perseverance and are hard-won. Our children know that we get better at things when we practice.

Self-Observation and Transformation

Self-observation is a tricky thing. First, we must learn to be objective, honest and forgiving. It is easier to do this with everyone else in our lives than with ourselves—that is another story! "If only I had tried harder. If only I had known. If only I had more time..." Sound familiar? How can we learn to look at ourselves as we would look at a stranger? How we perceive ourselves is like looking through a multi-colored screen that is always moving. We are not detached emotionally from ourselves, the situation or the outcome. How can we become an objective observer of ourselves? Again, this is not an easy task and takes time and practice.

When I was growing up my mother used to play a psychological game of baiting me into a conversation that would ultimately result in my becoming hysterical, out-of-control, screaming and crying. She would then sit and smile or laugh at me. I would flee to my room in a distraught state. Nothing was really gained from this dance; no one really won anything, but my mother retained control over my state of being. She never felt sorry for what she did and would go on as if nothing had happened. We all got our own brand of dysfunctional treatment from her.

At age 17, on the advice of our family doctor who knew my parents well and was treating me for the possible beginnings of an ulcer, I began therapy with a counselor. To say that I was under stress is putting it mildly! During therapy I began to realize how much of my own self-destructive behavior was due to the influence of my crazy mother. Next time I caught myself in the middle of one of her dances, I left the room before it hit its peak. Eventually I could recognize a situation in which this emotional interaction would start and could stop it before it started by removing myself from the line of fire. One day, many years later, I was able to disengage from her when she tried to play these psychological games.

We cannot change our parents, but we can choose to change ourselves. By doing so we can often initiate a change in the relationship with our own parents, children, spouse or partner. But it is hard work, and one can fall down many times on the path to transformation. The point is to get up and keep at it; one day we will reach the goal.

Then comes the next challenge! Until the end our days on earth, we are always learning. Unless we can acknowledge our own role in a problem we can never hope to achieve any real change. Moving the furniture around feels like change, but it is still just the same old stuff with a new name or location. Real transformation takes honest struggle with ourselves. There has to be a time when we, as adults, decide to become responsible for ourselves, to grow up and stop blaming others for our shortcomings. When our children or students perceive this process in us (and they always do), it will give them hope that they, too, have the potential to change themselves. They have the chance to be forgiven for their wrongdoings and mistakes and can become better people. This process of transformation cannot be measured in a physical way. Steiner called this process a "supersensible" experience; without being physically visible, nonetheless it is powerfully perceptible. Often it shows in the growing confidence and light in the person's eyes. As educators and parents we know that we are on the right track when a child finally achieves a goal, makes progress or turns to us with that look of understanding about him/herself.

It is very important to recognize and understand how human beings influence each other. What we know in our day-consciousness is the smallest part of reality. What stands behind the physically perceptible are profound and powerful forces which can be used either for furthering the well-being of ourselves and others or may be used to control and create negativity. It is a matter of choice in which direction we use our own forces.

Often when talking to a parent or teacher about the needs of children in his or her care, a moment comes when the "penny drops," that "Aha!" moment of recognition and understanding. The veil is lifted and the eyes of the soul finally perceive the truth. This moment can be a relief, but it can also be painful. To realize our mistakes, misperceptions and errors in a moment of truth offers us the possibility to change ourselves. It is the lot of human beings to learn by making mistakes and even causing pain for others by our actions. By recognizing what we have done, we are given the opportunity to wake up to our responsibility and to change ourselves to remedy the error. This process is all too human and we have a lifetime to practice it.

Until one is committed, there is hesitancy, the chance to draw back, always ineffectiveness. Concerning all acts of initiative (and creation), there is one elementary truth—the ignorance of which kills countless ideas and splendid plans: The moment one definitely commits oneself, then Providence moves, too. All sorts of things occur to help one that would never otherwise have occurred. A whole stream of events issues from the decision, raising in one's favor all manner of unforeseen incidents and material assistance, which no man could have dreamed would have come his way.

Whatever you can do, or dream you can, begin it. Boldness has genius, power and magic in it. Begin it now![13]

Steiner speaks about the Pedagogical Law in his book *Curative Education*, a series of twelve lectures given in 1924.[14] This rich and informative book reveals many important elements about the incarnation, development and education of children. In the second lecture (June 26, 1924), Dr. Steiner speaks with deep insight into the "supersensible" aspect of the teacher's effect upon his/her students, beyond what is taught in the lesson.[15] This process, called the *Pedagogical Law*,[16] takes place regardless of whether the teacher or the students are conscious of its effect. It is who we are that teaches and educates our children. It is not what we say but how we say it. One can use all kinds of fancy words, but children perceive the hidden intentions harbored within the adult; this has its impact upon the soul and body of the child.

Here we encounter a law, of the working of which we have abundant evidence throughout all education. It is as follows. Any one member of the human being is influenced by the next higher member (from whatever quarter it approaches) and only under such influence can that member develop satisfactorily. Thus, whatever is to be effective for the development of the physical body must be living in the etheric body—in an etheric body. Whatever is to be effective for the development of an astral body must be living in an ego, and an ego can be influenced only by what is living in a spirit-self. I could continue and go beyond the spirit-self, but there we should be entering the field of esoteric instructions.

What does this mean in practice? If you find that the etheric body of a child is in some way weakened or deficient, you must form and modify your own astral body in such a way that it can work upon the etheric body of the child, correcting and amending it. We could, in fact, make a diagram to demonstrate how this principle works in education.

Child	Teacher	Terminology
Physical Body	Etheric Body	Physical and Life Bodies
Etheric Body	Astral Body	Soul Body
Astral Body	Ego	Individuality
Ego	Spirit-Self	Higher Self

The teacher's etheric body (and this should follow quite naturally as a result of his training) must be able to influence the physical body of the child, and the teacher's astral body, the etheric body of the child. The ego of the teacher must be able to influence the physical body or the astral body of the child. And now you will be rather taken aback, for we come next to the spirit-self of the teacher, and you will be thinking that surely the spirit-self is not yet developed. Nevertheless, such is The Law. The spirit-self of the teacher must work upon the ego of the child... Education is indeed veiled in many mysteries.[17]

What was of great concern to Steiner was the effect of the teacher's astral body—the soul forces of thinking, feeling and willing, sympathies and antipathies—upon the etheric body or life forces of the child. This is also an important issue for parents, especially the primary caregiver. "The astral body of the teacher must be of such a character and quality that he is able to have an instinctive understanding for whatever debilities there may be in the child's etheric body. By ridding him/herself of every trace of subjective reaction, the teacher educates his or her own astral body."[18]

Again we come to the most important interplay between child and adult. It is a profound process, and the responsibility for the outcome rests on the self-development and education of the adult, not the child. Everything we do positively or negatively directly affects the karma (destiny) of the child. Whatever karmic obstacles the child has to face in this life can be lessened or even removed through proper care and education exercised from early childhood until adulthood. This does not mean that we should take away all challenges or enable the child by being over-indulgent. We should guide the child towards ever-growing age-appropriate independence. At the same time, we must strive to unconditionally validate with all due respect the individual essence of the person before us. Young children begin to learn through their first educators—their parents. What a marvelous and challenging destiny it is to be a parent!

We affect one another in many ways, not all of which are at first perceivable on the surface. But moods, unspoken agendas, thoughts/feelings and intentions are imprinted into the souls and even into the physical bodies of developing young children. Many struggles we encounter as adults have their origins in childhood. Children who are censored from expressing themselves in early childhood will have difficulty speaking up for themselves as adults. Let us not pass our own struggles onto our children or students.

Parents and teachers say this about children, "He pushes my buttons!"

I say, "But they are *your* buttons. You are the one who has to figure out how to disengage or heal the buttons in yourself so that they cannot be pushed. Unplug your energy from being manipulated by others, no matter who they are." A change in the consciousness and behavior of a parent will often have a direct effect upon the child. This is also true for a teacher in the classroom.

Many years ago a kindergarten assistant in a public school shared with me that a five-year-old boy was driving her crazy. He would follow her everywhere, make funny faces at her, poke her in the arm, leg or backside every chance he got, and try to touch her face. The boy was solid in build, with a beautiful round head, dark brown eyes and tan-colored skin. He moved around the room and sat in a chair like a little bear that was happy in his body, but was still trying to figure out how it all worked. His bright, dark eyes observed everything and he radiated happiness.

I shared my observations with the teacher's aide, suggesting that she create little daily tasks or jobs in the classroom, such as scrubbing the tables, folding the napkins, moving the furniture, carrying heavy objects to different places in the room or doing art projects that could include other children, such as cleaning up the toys or art supplies. Singing and making a playful mood around the activity would help. This child wanted her attention and her validation, to be seen and loved. If she took the initiative to draw him into activities with her, he would receive the things he needed, and she would have a good helper.

I did not visit this particular classroom again for two weeks, but when I did, the aide came to me and said, "I did everything you said and now this child is my favorite boy in the classroom! He is my buddy and he has learned so much even in the last two weeks!" She was able to share her positive qualities and help this little child in a way that turned her life around in the classroom. Many other children also benefited from this change in perspective, when she changed herself.

It is important to remember that not everything in our adult lives has be explained, analyzed or shared with our children. Today children of all ages are exposed to too much information that is not appropriate for them, information they are not able to digest and understand. Consequently, children are often anxious about many things to which they have been exposed and of which the parent is unaware. Also, children, babies too, hear, see and perceive the supersensible far more than adults know. As adults we must be more awake and conscious of what we are, who we are in every aspect of our lives and how we impact our children. It can be scary when the light of realization comes on within us. It is often our children and the effect our behavior is having on them that are our best and most effective teachers. We are looking, but are we seeing the truth? That is the important question to ask ourselves and then do something about. It takes courage and honesty.

Guilt has no place in parenting. Remorse leads us to awaken to ourselves and gives us the possibility to say, "This is my fault and I will strive to be a better person and parent." Guilt is the "gift that keeps on giving" but in a bad way that only produces more negativity and does not help us to change. Guilt is the "buck" that gets passed down from generation to generation; it is self-perpetuating. It needs to stop here. Nothing will ever change, improve or transform through guilt. By recognizing our errors and taking responsibility for our own behavior, we can change ourselves and at the same time become great role models for our children.

Dealing with Anger

One of the most damaging forces in childhood is anger. This is an all too human emotion, and how we express it and deal with it is the issue in parenting. When a parent is "on the boil" all the time or reacts to many daily events with anger, he or she is creating a quality of unease and fear in the children and spouse. This type of control over the family has devastating consequences. The entire family is held emotionally and physically hostage, and everyone becomes afraid to be themselves or to be trusting in this environment. Everyone becomes a victim. The perpetrator needs outside counseling in behavior management to help change this behavior. Many a child who acts aggressively or responds with anger in school often has an angry parent as a role model. The child cannot safely express him/herself at home, so it comes out at school where he/she feels safer. Anger can serve a positive purpose in helping us pull away from negative situations or in stopping something that is unhealthy for us. But when we meet children every day with anger, they never see its transformative qualities, only the negative effects.

The National Center for Prosecution of Child Abuse (NCPCA) has developed guidelines for parents and teachers for communicating with children.[19] These suggestions are intended to help adults stop and think before reacting with anger or aggression towards children. Again, the responsibility is placed at the feet of the perpetrator, the person with the anger response.

1. Reward children; compliment them when they do well. Instead of telling them, "No-no, do not do that!" tell them what they should be doing.
2. When pressure builds up, do not lash out at your child(ren) in anger.
3. Control your temper. Never act in anger.
4. If your own childhood was unhappy and unpredictable, consider professional counseling and/or a parenting class to bolster self-esteem and promote coping skills.
5. Do not worry about being the perfect parent. It's not possible.

6. Remember, you are the adult. Set a good example.
7. Praise your child daily in some way. Kind words will make him or her feel special today and help him or her be a better adult tomorrow.

What is common sense to some is not for others. We can fall into patterns of behavior which have a devastating impact on family, friends, coworkers and ourselves. We must first become aware of what we are doing and then have the intention and desire to change. Many successful strategies and guidelines have been integrated and spelled out in a plethora of parent advice books. Many good self-help support books, tapes and groups are available to assist in this process. But all the help in the world will not avail if the person engaged in the behavior does not want to change.

Observing Your Child

A Non-judgmental Approach to Observing Your Child

Many years ago, as a student at Emerson College in England, I had the great privilege of working with Dutch botanist Fritz Julius. In his botany course we studied the Goethean approach to observing nature. We learned to quiet ourselves, withholding all judgment and opinion in our observation in order to create a space for the phenomena to speak their truths, their secrets. This was an amazing process, and the outcome created a deeper experience of the true nature of the plant in gesture, color, form and substance. I learned to "take in nature" rather than label and analyze everything without really "seeing" the object being observed. We learned how to look from the whole gesture and environment of the plant to the part and then back again to the whole. In each little part lies the seed, germ and essence of the whole.

When I returned to the United States and began working with children again, I applied the same principles and techniques to the observation of children. This has proved to be amazingly helpful in figuring out the real needs of children and "what stands behind mere appearances." Labeling children tends to stop the process of understanding. As soon as we stop observing and begin to fill ourselves with facts and labels, we are in danger of not seeing the truth. When we fill the space with our own opinions or knowledge, we increase the possibility of missing the most important elements in the child. The "whole child approach" in education means that we strive to never lose sight of the entire child, even when focusing on one aspect or part.

Human beings are unique and special. But there are developmental and learning milestones and phases that we all go through around the same age. This is the baseline that we, as educators and parents, use to determine how a child is doing, how he or she is progressing toward a growing independence and maturity. Many things are taken into account and weighed against the child's individual karma and unique being. A detailed family history helps to fill out the heredity and environmental picture of the child's life, both of which have a powerful impact upon his or her growth and development.

Below is a simple checklist of areas for learning how to observe children. The most important element is the observer, who must first start his/her own process to create objectivity, to allow space in the observing, and to allow time for the child to establish trust and begin to reveal him/ herself.

Physical Description: Height, weight, shape of head, face, nose, ears, complexion, hair color and quality, trunk form and proportions, legs, feet and arches, hands—shape and constitution (warm/cold/dry/damp, and so forth). The observer can already see heredity at work and, at the same time, the individuality of the child begin to emerge.

Description of Movement: Control, strength and muscle tone, mood when moving; origin, isolation and speed of movement; gesture, facial expression, and gaze; bending/leaning, posture; intention and motor planning, and so forth. In the movement of the child in many different situations, the observer can determine how comfortable the child feels in his/her body and how he/she is able to plan, anticipate, balance and safely express him/herself in gesture and walk. Many intimate aspects are revealed in our movements. When a child does not like to move, this is also an important observation and needs to be explored further.

Description of Speech: Pitch, tone, intensity, articulation, flow of breathing, comprehensibility, modulation, speech disturbances, origin—nasal, throaty, slurred or clear, rushed, and so forth. Speech is unique to human beings. How we express ourselves through the spoken word is noteworthy and reveals many things about ourselves.

Description of Behavior: How the child behaves in school, with adults, with peers, in a large group, small group, one-on-one, during class or free time; if the child is restless, able to come to quiet, and so forth. Behavior is a symptom of something and not the cause. Always observe behavior and then ask the question, "Why does the child need to behave in this way?" What is the cause of the behavior? Are we reacting to or addressing the symptom or the cause? Often a child is misdiagnosed and an incorrect treatment recommended because only the behavior was perceived and not the cause of the behavior.

Description of Faculties:
- *Perceiving, processing, understanding, following through with intention*—Orientation in time, space; thinking patterns; reproduces/creates; fantasy, memory; practical intelligence; capacity for representation
- *Feeling*—Sense of reality, enthusiasm, emotions, empathy or lack of it, fears, social behavior, asks for help, and so forth
- *Willing/action*—Instinctive behavior, impulses, anxieties, interference in or motives for activity, capacity for beginning and ending work, will to learn, courage to act, and so forth

Description of Nutrition and Eating: Likes and dislikes, digestion, proper chewing of food, sensitivities to tastes and textures of food, timing, setting, manners, company, and so forth.

Description of Sleep: How the child sleeps, how much, any difficulties including any issues about the quality or quantity of sleep; does the child get up many times in the night, sleeping in a "family bed," and so forth.

Recognizing What Is You and What Is Your Child

Sometimes the "family dance" or dynamic is so well-orchestrated and practiced that no one realizes what is really going on. Everyone in the family gets caught in the dance and becomes a victim. Children are masters at negotiating, almost from birth, to get what they need. This can evolve into a power play to get what they want. What a child wants on the surface is not necessarily what he/she really needs on the inside. Often children who argue at home, throw temper tantrums, yell, fight or hit out are actually asking for the adults to take charge. Children who behave this way are unhappy and miserable; they do not want to be out of control. Something in them knows they are not getting what they really need and so they demand attention and reaction through negative behavior. Many parents today are afraid of their own children who behave this way and back off even further, thus perpetuating the cycle of negative behavior.

Creating Healthy Attachments and Bonding

The patterns of parent-child attachments, researched and documented in a wide variety and number of books on child development, are established in infancy.[20] Overall, seventy percent of attachments fall into the category of secure attachments between parent and child. The children display a healthy balance between independent play and exploration and maintaining proximity to the caregiving parent. One sees the toddler explore the environment and then look to the parent for reassurance and encouragement. Secure children are animated, happy, and creative and learn independent skills which can be generalized as they grow older.

In contrast, the anxiously-attached child is unable to form a secure attachment with the caregiver. These children fall into two pattern groups: One is the anxious-resistant attachment and the other is the anxious-avoidant attachment. Resistant children readily seek contact with the caregiver but seem restless, hypersensitive, even cranky or fussy. They do not respond well to comforting or calming. There is often a resistance to the closeness they need or crave. The anxious-avoidant child readily detaches from the mother or caregiver and appears not to be wary around strangers or cry when the mother is not present. These children actually avoid the care-giving parent by turning away, not making eye contact or ignoring her altogether. This behavior often occurs after a long absence of the parent and becomes more pronounced after a second separation. Children can become very upset and act out as a response to breaking the bond. As stress increases, the more avoidant behavior appears in the child. The child remains in a heightened agitated state even after the absent parent returns.

The bonding process and the forming of healthy, secure attachments begin at birth. All of the nurturing through touch, closeness, nursing, rocking and gentle, loving words builds a bond between the mother and infant. When this is not established early, the anxious behaviors can arise. The intentions of surrounding adults become imprinted into the soul of the infant or small child. This is not readily perceived by most people, especially if they are absorbed in themselves and do not pay attention to the effects of their behavior. But it all is reflected through the response behavior of the child. Disturbances in bonding and attachments take time to heal; the child needs daily repatterning to build trust and security.

What Stands behind the Behavior?

Often what we recognize as a behavior problem is only the symptom, not the cause of the problem, but the product. To find the cause, we need to look for what stands behind the presenting behavior. A ready example of this is ADHD, attention deficit hyperactive disorder. First of all, this diagnosis covers many issues related to attention or lack of attention in children of all ages. Often the treatment is drugs. But what causes the behavior? There are many reasons, one of which is allergies or sensitivities to pollutants and chemicals in the environment.

A little boy in second grade had great difficult staying in his seat, standing in the morning circle, or being in a line of children. He was unable to come to quiet, to focus on his work or control his anxious behavior. This had been evident since kindergarten. His disruptive behavior was

63

caused by severe allergies. He was sensitive to so many things that he almost seemed to be allergic to himself. He was not at home in his body, and his body did not give him the foundation for learning. He had to use a great amount of energy to stay seated and focused on his assignments. To expect this boy to control his behavior was not reasonable.

Standing in line in a coffee shop, a dad was being served while his little four- or five-year-old son was standing next to him making demands about what he wanted. The father responded by asking him, would he like this, would he like that, and so on. The boy became increasingly agitated and finally hit his father two or three times in the leg and yelled, "You're not listening to me!" His father looked at him and then at me. He was totally bewildered as to how to respond to this behavior.

I wanted to say, "Step back from the counter, take your son to the side and deal with this behavior." But I was there only for a cup of coffee, not to interfere into parenting dynamics. So many parents are confronted with this same behavior from their children, and it all starts when the children are young.

The behavior children display can be melancholy, anger, aggression, opposition, and so forth, and can be motivated by a need not only in the child, but actually also in the parent, to be loved or acknowledged. It can stem from a co-dependent relationship in which no one is healthy. The parent needs the child to remain dependent upon him/her to the point that the growing child feels suffocated. Or, the other side of the coin is a parent who ignores the needs of the child, forcing the child to demand attention with bad behavior. Breaking this pattern is challenging but important for the health of the entire family. The person who has the power to address the real needs that stand behind the behavior is the parent.

A seventh grade teacher in Zurich, Switzerland, asked for help with one of her students, who doodled constantly all over his notebooks and book covers. She had already tried offering to reward him with a new binder if he would stop, but he could not stop himself because the cause of the behavior was not addressed. I suggested that she teach him or have the art teacher teach him how to do black and white shaded drawing. The child needed to draw to help himself stay focused in class, and the shaded drawing technique offered him a rhythmical method which could replace the doodling and be not so distracting or destructive. He was also given a special notebook to draw in and a special pen and pencil. In less than a week, the student stopped doodling in his books and eventually did not need to draw all the time to help him focus in class. His teacher took him in to town and bought him a new binder as she had promised.

A dedicated nursery teacher was concerned about a sweet five-year-old girl in her class, who sucked her thumb at different times throughout the morning. She also sub-vocalized while playing, felt more comfortable chatting with the teacher and aide instead of the other children, and needed additional time to enter into the activities of the class. The teacher met with the parents and gave them various strategies to help their daughter stop sucking her thumb.

I observed this child for a half hour in her classroom and then met with the teacher. I explained that this little girl was very open and sensitive to everything going on around her. She was young and became anxious easily, but she had developed a very effective strategy for coping with her anxieties: sucking her thumb to self-soothe. She also expressed outwardly her inner process. Her sub-vocalizing could be guided into conversation and would gradually occur less as she felt more secure in her body and surroundings. Her little soul needed connection with adults.

I also suggested that it was important not to take away sucking her thumb but to create other ways of self-soothing by strengthening her senses of touch, life, self-movement and balance. To force the child to stop sucking her thumb would impose an adult agenda, a far cry from meeting or honoring the child where she really was. Sucking her thumb and sub-vocalizing did not mean that something was wrong; the child was showing us what was happening inside her and what she really needed.

There are many ways to view and act upon behavior issues that arise at home and in school. It is our responsibility to develop our skills of observation and perception so that we can recognize what stands behind the behavior. Then we must look for a solution that will rightly address the needs of the child and lead to the appropriate remediation. Children are resilient. When they receive the help that is truly needed, they know in themselves that it is right. Children show us that what we are doing is correct when we see them become happier and begin to change.

> *Ring the bells that still can ring*
> *Forget your perfect offering*
> *There's a crack in everything*
> *That's how the light gets in!* [21]
> – Leonard Cohen

RECOGNIZING AND MEETING
THE NEEDS OF CHILDREN

Your children are not your children!
They are the sons and daughters
Of life's longing for itself.
They come through you, but not from you,
And though they are with you
Yet they belong not to you.[22]
— Kahlil Gibran, 1883–1931

Unconditional Love and Validation

Whenever I give a workshop or a lecture to parents and teachers I begin by saying, "Raise your hand if you would like to be unconditionally validated by at least one person in your life." And all of the hands go up! This is the one most important experiences in our lives. We can bear most every personal hardship if we know that one person unconditionally validates us, lock, stock, and barrel, the whole of us in our entirety. This means that this person loves the good and the bad, and all of our imperfections and faults in between. If we feel this way as adults, just imagine how a child feels! Think back to yourself as a child and remember longing to be recognized, for someone to see who you really were. Children want to see our eyes light up with acknowledgement when they come into the room. This is the key to the kingdom, and with it there is no door that will remain closed to experience and learning.

In the first Waldorf school in Stuttgart, Steiner would speak at the all-school assembly and ask the students, "Do you love your teachers?" The children would shout, "Yes!" He would instill in the children an awareness of the wonderful education they were receiving from their dedicated teachers and their loving parents. At the end of the school year he would say, "We will be back in the fall to learn to do good work, to develop our souls to be strong for life, and to awaken our spirit to true humanity." Thus, he instilled in the children and teachers a deep validation of human importance and a commitment to true humanity and love.

Through validation of ourselves and others we rise up another level of consciousness to our true selves. Everyone benefits from this activity. "Unconditional" means what it says—without reservation, no strings attached. "I will love you, if..." is not validating! When we use words of love and validation in emotional blackmail, we are actually lying and teaching our children to do the same. There can be no trust or security there. Children are experts at sensing and seeing the lie in us. Often the deep, personal need to be loved overrides the lie, and we will do anything to be loved. This is also true for adults.

Sensory Protection

When else in history have human beings ever had to address the problem of sensory overload as we do today? Children used to walk to school, which allowed them time and activity to wake up and integrate into their bodies and senses before entering the classroom. They had time to socialize with friends and feel part of the fabric of the community. Today we find a totally different scenario.

Daily life is stressful for everyone, especially for children. Now we wake up in stress. Everyone rushes through breakfast, or eats it in the car on the way to school, or skips it altogether. We are living a drive-by lifestyle and the more affluent a family, the more often this dynamic can happen. It seems as if the more we have, the less we have! Children need nurturing, not things or possessions. The more cluttered our lives have become, the less we are paying attention to what really matters.

Numerous mainstream studies have been conducted on the effects of overstimulating the senses, especially the visual and

68

auditory senses of children of all ages. The effects of television, movies, radio, computers, gameboys, iPods and the like have physiological and psychological ramifications for all of us, but most of all for our children.

Years ago someone told me of a study on the effects of television on first grade students. In this study, two classrooms of thirty-one students each were given a variety of tasks to do for one month: One group was to watch one hour of television before school, while the other would see no television before school. This was arranged through the parents. Reading assessments were given to both groups at the beginning and the end of the month to compare the impact of watching television before school on reading ability and performance. At the end of the first month the results were dramatic: All of the children in the TV group had dropped in their reading scores, even the good readers; in the second group, all of the reading scores had improved, some dramatically. Then the groups were switched, and, at the end of the second month, the results were the same. This is only one example of the negative impact of television on child development.

The use of television and computers has dramatically increased over the last ten years, and is still increasing! Technology is getting faster, more refined, smaller and more streamlined, and with increasing devastating impact on the brain and our senses. Damage is being done through radiation which comes from everything electronic. What are we doing to protect our children and ourselves from injury from long-term use of technology? What was supposed to be providing us modern conveniences so that we would have more time to do other things has done just the opposite. Modern human beings are in a state of hyper-drive and suffer from technology-based addictions! Is this what we want for our children and for ourselves? Children are being traumatized by the media.

A second grade boy, whose mother insisted that he never watched television, drew a picture of a person, a house and a tree. The person in the picture was a pirate. When asked, "What kind of a person did you draw?" the child replied, "This is a pirate." When asked how he knew what a pirate looked like, he said, "I saw it in a movie." "Did you see the movie Hook?" *He said, "No it was a DVD movie of the* Pirates of the..." *I said, "The Caribbean?" and he said that it was.*

The images imprinted on this little boy were ones he could not process or make sense of and had a powerful effect upon his soul. There is not a kindergarten or grades teacher in the world who does not learn on Monday what her students have seen or been exposed to on the weekend because they need to—and do—talk about it and play it out to try make sense of it or get it out of their system. The more sensitive the child is, the more fantasy-rich and impressionable, and the deeper these impressions imprint into the child's soul. This activity can affect even their physical health. Children are impressionable and vulnerable. They cannot always tell us what is going on or what leads them to have nightmares or become afraid to go to sleep. The parent must be the guard at the door of the child's senses and soul. We must protect the child from these addictive, deadening forces. Observe children and you will see the effects technology has on them.

There is documented scientific evidence suggesting the possibility of brain damage caused by the use of cell phones held to the ear. Hearing loss has been recorded at younger ages from the use of iPods and high definition sound systems. It has been long known that radiation from computers is not healthy for adults. What is it doing to children? Attention deficits and short-term attention spans caused by the early exposure to television viewing were in the news twenty years ago. "Sesame Street" has been linked to the development in the children who watch regularly a 7–10 second attention span as a direct result of the visual images being on the screen for 7–10 seconds. What it must be today! Not to mention the corporate brainwashing of children, teaching them through potent visual advertising images how to be consumers at an ever-earlier age. Please, if this is progress, let's slow it down!

One father told me recently that when his wife first decided it would be in their children's best interest to turn off the television altogether, he felt dubious and unhappy. He enjoyed watching television after a long day at work, but the children became "glued to the tube" and argumentative when it was turned off. Once the television was shut away, he began to experience an amazing change in his children. They began to play inside and outside; their creativity and intelligence emerged. He was flabbergasted at the heightened quality of their conversations and their new-found willingness to do chores and be part of a family. Everyone in the household was happier, and parenting these three wonderful children became a joy.

Feeling Safe and Secure

Why are our children today experiencing increased anxiety, nervousness and depression? Our children stand before us as engaging mysteries. They may exhibit restlessness, a strong sense of self and imagination or be challenged by clumsiness or health issues. Our task as concerned adults is to find ways to understand them and provide for them in our homes and classrooms, to remove hindrances to their unfolding, and to form relationships with them. We can improve our understanding of children by considering child development from various perspectives: physical, energy/time qualities, soul and ego/self.

To help us create healthy environments for growing children, we can explore the relationship between the development of the lower or foundation senses and the various emotional disturbances which can be present as anxiety, fear, and disruptive behavior in the young child and as depression as the child gets older. The roots of the behavioral problems may lie in early childhood. Once the source of the presenting behavior is identified, the cause can be addressed, remediated and even healed. Many teachers and therapists in

Waldorf remedial education work out of Steiner's indications in this area. Two additional valuable resources are Audrey McAllen's work *The Extra Lesson*[23] and *Working with Anxious, Nervous, and Depressed Children, A Spiritual Perspective to Guide Parents* by Hennig Köhler (recently translated into English),[24] both of which address the development of these important senses. Mainstream sensory integration occupational therapists have worked with these principles with children of all ages.

What follows below is a summary of the material from these sources that I use in my lectures and workshops for parents and kindergarten teachers. My own observations and experiences with children are included.

The Four Foundation Senses which Promote a Healthy Sense of Security

The Sense of Life gives us a deep inner sense of one's own body and health, how we feel in our own bodies. A visceral sense, it is directly strengthened or compromised by the other eleven senses. Lack of proper nurturing, warmth, nutrition, physical and soul care, sleep, or play, or trauma, or verbal, mental or physical abuse or neglect all impact this foundation sense important for all human beings.

Disturbed Sense of Life: The disruptive, unruly, oppositional or aggressive child

- Behavior—unruly, nervous, hyperactive, disruptive, sad, whining, cranky. Child avoids stillness or quiet and tends to seek out stimulation (sometimes harmful) or is totally listless with no forces or stamina to do anything.
- Can be disruptive during quiet story, circle or nap-time and has difficulty settling down
- Displays poor appetite, difficulty going to sleep at night, restless sleep patterns
- Always in motion, restless, does not feel good in own body
- May develop tics, eye-blinking, foot tapping, facial grimace, or self-stimulation

- Not always aware of bodily needs, no sense of warmth or cold, but looks pale
- Is very sensitive, easily upset or wounded by others, and is often unaware of consequences of own behavior

Underlying Condition: Bodily fear is the underlying gesture, a fear of awakening to the body and a lack of a sense of well-being especially impacting sleep patterns. Disorientation in the body exists due to constitution or overstimulation by daily life. A feeling of being unwanted or abandoned is the underlying mood in many of these children, all of which is unconscious.

Important Inner Qualities for the Parent or Teacher
- A connection to the child's angel
- Helping the child develop a sense of reverence to all things leads to tolerance in later life.
- Attentiveness to the sense of life through:
  o Improved nutrition, bland not spicy, warm food
  o Warmth in body, soul and spirit
  o Rhythm, routine, ritual
  o Bodily care and comfort: contact, clothing, warm bath
  o Healthful sleep life: help child look back over the day
  o Reverence, attentiveness, patience, and active tolerance
  o Practice of the inner discipline of slowness, harmony
  o Basis for future moral life and capacity for tolerance

The Sense of Touch provides us with boundaries—"where I end and the outer world begins"—and the security of knowing that we are safe in our own bodies.

Disturbed Sense of Touch: The fearful, timid, worried child
- Lack of a sense of security
- Fear of new experiences and the future
- Fear of thresholds—going to bed at night, going to school, getting ready for school
- Tendency to get stuck in the familiar, to whine and manipulate to avoid what he/she does not want to do

- Often verbal, thin-skinned, pale
- Can be rich in fantasy and imagination
- Tendency to bronchitis, asthma, skin rashes, bladder infections
- Strong affinity to festivals, rituals, and beautiful things
- Difficulty creating social boundaries

Underlying Condition: Lack of sense of protection, suffers from a "soul wound," does not feel at home in his/her own body as a foundation for security in life, fears abandonment

Important Inner Qualities for the Parent or Teacher
- Deep pressure activities: massage, blanket wrap, joint compressions
- Care for the skin—oils, baths, touch
- Natural fiber clothing
- Cultivation of tactile sensing of qualities
- Protective gesture in early evening/bedtime
- Attitude of gentle firmness and form
- Devoted care of the environment through gardening, bedroom, house
- Conversations with the child about what is going to happen before it takes place, what will happen the next day, for example

The Sense of Movement is perceiving one's own movement, proprioception. **The Sense of Balance** is centeredness within one's self.

Disturbed Senses of Movement and Balance: The sad, withdrawn, dejected, brooding child
- Inability to move with the world
- Inability to freely imitate
- Difficulty in engaging in creative play with other children
- Inability to inwardly experience the imprinting of external sense impressions

- Lack of spontaneity, joy, flexibility or ability to conform
- Poor articulation, does not resonate within
- Clumsy movement
- Difficulty sitting in chair in class
- Wandering during circle, recess, games, looks "lost"
- Shocked when yelled at or dealt with in a strong manner
- Stranded in the midst of activity
- Panic if things get too hectic
- Inability to hold the thread in a conversation
- Sense of paralysis, helplessness or being excluded

Underlying Condition: Weakened ability to imitate. These children are easily overwhelmed by movement in the environment, by hectic and chaotic activity. They are unable to perceive inwardly, imitate, assimilate, integrate or understand what comes to them from others or the world. This makes socialization and play with others challenging. Balance is our sense of being centered in ourselves and safe, a place from which we can move with confidence and comfort. Children whose sense of balance has been disturbed lack the foundation for later socialization and the moral capacities of compassion, empathy, sensing the inner needs of others. They may be inwardly rigid or compulsive, concerned only with self and personal inner activity.

Important Inner Qualities for the Parent or Teacher
- Unsentimental empathy for everything and everyone
- Compassion as an active example for imitation
- Loving and patient attention to all that he/she does to help the child feel at peace and integrated in the body
- Genuine, active tolerance
- An environment of movement and activities that are worthy of imitation
- Meaningful, beautiful, clear, well-formed speech
- Meaningful, musical/rhythmical movement, and gesture
- Love expressed through the body towards the child, others, and the world

- Opportunities for play and free movement of arms and legs
- Games of balance/symmetry and spatial dynamics
- Practical activities of daily life that involve lifting heavy objects, baking bread, digging, proprioceptive stimulation, and so forth
- Opportunities for imitation
- Ordered, meaningful processes: for example, working with wool from carding to finished product, baking, cooking, modeling
- Music, recitation, dance

Summary

There is no such thing as a lazy, contrary or mean child by nature. Every child wants to learn, be successful and receive unconditional love and praise. All bodily sense-disturbed children display a lack of confidence and trust in their ability to ACT—these are disturbances of the WILL. All are inner senses which lay the foundation for subsequent moral and social development.

- Unruliness indicates a disturbed Sense of Life (well-being)
- Insecurity indicates a disturbed Sense of Touch
- A lack of inner understanding indicates disturbed Senses of Movement and Balance

Remember:
- Encouragement
- Unconditional validation and love
- Reverence for all things
- Confidence-building through accomplishing meaningful deeds
- Quiet mindfulness of the child's weakness(es) and what he/she cannot do, but not confrontational
- Acknowledgement of small successes and work with individual strengths
- Help in following through on all tasks and praise for accomplishment

- Transformation of "I can't" into "I will try"
- Recognition of the child's true incarnating self and earthly "chosen" karma
- Acknowledgement of the courage needed to face difficulties and to meet what is challenging
- Supportive working between teachers and parents
- Work with the child's angel
- Addressing the cause of the behavior, not the symptom

Home Program to Address Developmental Issues

Be creative! Remember to give your child time to practice these activities so they can learn and develop the skills properly. These activities include suggestions from a variety of resources including an occupational therapist, the Waldorf kindergarten and my own remedial and pedagogical work. Remember, children learn though play far more than adults realize. Let the innate wisdom of their play prevail and learn to play with them!

Activities for Vestibular Stimulation
1. Play with a large beach or Physio-ball, which the child can lie on top of, roll over, sit on, bounce, and so forth (with parent supervision)
2. Roll or slide in a cardboard box down a hill
3. Wheelbarrow rides
4. Jump on stepping stones or trampoline (beds are good too!)
5. Make use of playground equipment or backyard swing set: merry-go-round, slide, swing, teeter-totter, jungle gym, and so forth
6. Climb up stairs and jump with feet together
7. Swing in a hammock
8. Play jump rope games
9. Walk on a balance beam or thick rope
10. Rock on a balance or rocker board

Activities to Improve Tactile Perception
1. Exploration of a wide variety of textures: clay, sand, paint, and so forth

2. Kneading bread dough for baking
3. Deep pressure massage of feet, legs and back
4. "Burrito wrap," rolling the child in a blanket for deep pressure and calming
5. Firm pressure rubdowns after bathtime and before bedtime
6. "Treasure Box": Fill a large box with different sized beans, have child sit in the box and search with his/her fingers for treasures (thimble, shell, wooden animals, small doll, and so forth)
7. Drawing in the sand
8. Making angels in the snow, sand, or on a carpet
9. Carrying heavy bean bags or groceries when shopping; help with the wheelbarrow in the garden

Activities to Improve Gross Motor Skills
1. Crawl on all fours through hula hoops, under tables and chairs, and so forth
2. Hit a balloon on a string
3. Swimming
4. Shake sheets and towels out for spreading or folding
5. Drawing or writing upright on a chalkboard or easel
6. Household chores: carrying dishes or heavy objects, moving furniture, sweeping, vacuuming, washing windows, raking, shoveling, and so forth
7. The Zoo exercises
8. Crawling and creeping
9. "Simon Says"
10. "Follow the Leader"
11. Twister game
12. Balloon volleyball
13. Tug of war
14. Hula hoop
15. Making angels in the snow, sand or on a carpet
16. Jumping games and jumping rope
17. Swinging and climbing

Activities for Developing Skills of Perception

1. Sorting beads, cards, buttons and shells by size, shape, and color
2. Sorting laundry (socks)
3. Copying designs with various objects and media
4. Playing songs and games that emphasize body parts, "Hokey Pokey," for example
5. Singing songs with hand movements ("Itsy Bitsy Spider")
6. Using and acting out spatial concepts, such as big/small, over/under, in/out, up/down, forward/back, and so forth
7. Painting and drawing
8. Playing with wooden blocks, Lincoln Logs, Legos
9. Jumping over a rope and other objects
10. Playing various board games: "Chutes and Ladders," "Candyland"

Activities for Developing Skills for Daily Life

1. Tube socks come before heel socks.
2. Buttons, ties, zippers on a doll or pocketbook come before child practices on own clothes, and big buttons come before small buttons.
3. Dress-up with costumes
4. The child can hold small objects while pushing his arms through the sleeves so fingers do not get stuck.
5. Talk about what you are doing as you help your child get dressed.
6. Allow enough time for your child to dress and undress.
7. Encourage your child to independently do all daily activities which are age-appropriate: sweeping, raking, shoveling, digging, folding laundry, washing dishes, polishing, setting the table, making beds, and so forth.
8. Help with grocery shopping, picking things out and carrying them, pushing the cart, putting things away at home

Activities for Developing Visual Motor Skills

1. Paintbrush or giant chalk on a slanted surface (chalkboard) or on paper on a wall or easel
2. Scissors
3. String beads, macaroni, straws, paper clips, and other materials
4. Squirt bottles
5. Eye dropper with colored tissue paper to stick on clear contact paper
6. Sort beads or beans
7. Finger knitting
8. Pinching clothespins with thumb and fingertips
9. Tiddlywinks
10. Form drawing, tracing shapes
11. Swings and monkeybars for climbing
12. Kneading and rolling dough into small balls, using a rolling pin to flatten dough
13. Helping to peel and chop vegetables and fruit
14. Catching and throwing various balls
15. Cutting and pasting

Fine Motor and Eye-Hand Coordination Activities

1. Kneading dough and mixing batter to make bread or cookies
2. Finger knitting (also prepares children for proper knitting in first grade)
3. Beginning sewing with large needles and yarn on felt, and gradually moving to finer work and cross stitch
4. Stacking and playing with blocks; the more natural the textures and materials, the more creative expression for the children. (This also promotes many skills including the sense of touch and balance.)
5. Sorting and stringing beads or beans
6. Folding paper and clothes
7. Marble games played with hands (shooting marbles through targets) and marble pickup with feet and toes

8. Finger games (also for dexterity)
9. Finger puppets great for imaginative play (and dexterity)
10. Using scissors to cut different types of paper (also helps develop muscle control and pressure)
11. Making paper fans, cards, airplanes, snowflakes (Children love these activities.)
12. Dressing and undressing dolls
13. Building with hammer and nails
14. Drawing and painting

DISCIPLINE AND HEALTHY BOUNDARIES

The Need for Boundaries:
Do They Help or Hinder Child Development?

This is an important reality in our lives from early childhood through to the end of our lives. Even as adults we experience how challenging it is when we live or work with someone who does not have established boundaries. What do we experience? This type of person comes toward us like a tidal wave, flows over and around us with seemingly no sense of our separate being. He/she interrupts and is unaware of breaking into a conversation or a train of thought. This person tends to stand very close and is always "in your face." Exhibiting this disrespectful behavior, the person often does not realize that he/she is doing anything inappropriate.

What happens with children? Without boundaries a child is like a house with no outer walls to provide safety, structure, form, stability or protection so that rhythm, breathing, quiet and good health can exist within. Without clear boundaries established by adults to provide routine, rhythm and ritual, then chaos fills the space. Children will take over and run the show, often becoming demanding, cranky, uncooperative, and oppositional; they throw temper tantrums, and even become physically and/or verbally abusive to siblings and parents.

Today there are many popular media programs to help parents "get it together" and provide practical suggestions for bringing the household back into order and harmony. A particularly helpful resource is *Family First* by Phil McGraw, MD, which provides practical advice to parents on dealing with family issues.[25]

Positive Aspects of Setting Healthy Boundaries
- Creates a sense of security and builds trust in self and others
- Gives a feeling of safety and reduces anxiety
- Leads to self-control over behavior
- Helps to develop a sense of self as both a separate individual and a member of the family group
- Builds an awareness of where the individual ends and the outer world begins
- Leads to the growing development of healthy self-control and self-esteem
- Takes the burden of authority off children in the early years and allows them to be children and not hyper-vigilant as adults. (The parent or teacher needs to carry that responsibility.)

Negative Aspects of Not Having Healthy Boundaries
- A child-controlled home is not a happy household. A child without personal boundaries is a challenging student in the classroom.
- Strict control from others does not lead to healthy self-control. Too much control or ridged boundaries can be restrictive, suffocating and cause lack of trust, weakening a sense of self-reliance.
- Frequent or constant criticism from others of our actions creates fear and anxiety and teaches children to be critical of self and others.

The Double-Edged Sword:
When Are Boundaries Healthy or too Restrictive?

It is always challenging to bring ourselves and our environment into balance. Questions need to be considered. Are these boundaries too much/too restrictive or are they too little/too loose? Finding a balance between freedom and control is a challenge. But we cannot establish a healthy sense of responsible freedom without a healthy sense of self-control.

Children learn early how to negotiate with adults to get their own way, but in reality everyone loses. Adults ought not get in the habit of negotiating, for children are much better at this game. Their temper tantrums and "hissy" fits are often a type of power play to control the situation. Remember, all tantrums need an audience. It is impossible to resolve a problem when a child or teen is in this state. But the adult does not have to stand by and watch or be abused. Step out of the ring!

Creating appropriate, healthy boundaries and letting the child breathe, experiment and explore his/her own unique abilities allow for room to be creative. When a family takes the time to be together to do things, children learn from their parents as role models. Is what a child sees on the outside the same as what is going on in the inside of their parents? When does too much nurturing become disabling or detrimental to the children's developing their independent skills and abilities—nursing; staying in the family bed; doing personal care and daily chores for children well beyond the time they should learn to do them for themselves? Often children will turn on the over-indulgent parent, even hating him or her for making them so dependent.

Setting Healthy Boundaries for Our Children:
Who Is in Charge?

We are living in a time when most of us feel rushed, over-scheduled, stressed and unable to breathe. Most of us have taken multitasking to an all-time high. But what are we missing in the process? If we feel stressed, what do our children experience? How are they coping with the "lack of time"? How does this type of modern lifestyle affect their abilities to learn and communicate, and what is the impact on their behavior and health?

One practical way to help our children develop a healthy sense of will is by setting age-appropriate boundaries. This section addresses how to reduce stress through strengthening daily rhythms and making healthier lifestyle choices.

The Inner Nature of the Will

The inner nature of the will is very deep in a visceral sense. The will comprises forces that give us the power to act. When we connect these forces with our ego consciousness, we have the power to change the very substance of our own being. When a child's will forces, which come from a common wellspring and are not yet individualized, are set in motion for the good, the child experiences health through his or her whole being. The rightness of an action is clear to a child not only from its outcome, but also by how it feels inwardly. How do we help our children develop a healthy sense of will?

Children today need strong will forces to survive the challenging times that we live in and to develop the courage to stand up to the obstacles and overcome them. If we do not help them develop a healthy sense of will—always in the service of growth, development, truth, beauty and goodness—the child will become isolated in a negative experience of willfulness. When the will forces are used only for self-gratification and gain (the modern credo), we become disconnected from the universal. This is devastating for children. They become unhappy, moody and oppositional. They lose the joy of childhood, becoming self-critical and critical of others. Temper tantrums and other behavioral issues can arise when the will forces, which play out through the feelings, are not addressed by the parents and teachers in the appropriate manner. During childhood the foundation stones and habits are imprinted into each of us which will grow and develop into free, moral qualities in adulthood. What a child misses in this regard in childhood will surface with devastating repercussions in pre- or full adolescence.

How Can We Give Our Children a Healthy Childhood?

The foundations for a strong, creative will, one which is based on goodness and truth, begin with the adults' providing healthy examples and role models who are worthy of imitation. We must learn to "walk the talk" and not just know these principles in our heads. We have the power to change the flow and habits of our family and classroom by changing ourselves first, and then helping our children. We must learn to set routines and boundaries for ourselves and our children. Everything does matter in childhood! How many of us spend years overcoming what happened or did not happen to us in childhood? Life is difficult enough. Let us work to cultivate the garden of the will to serve the growing individual and the world in a positive way, enabling the future adult to be prepared to make successful choices out of freedom, choices based on a deep sense of what is right and wrong.

What Are Your Memories of Childhood?

- Traditions: festivals, family vacations, Sunday dinner together, going to the opening game of the Red Sox, and the like
- Daily and yearly rituals: bedtime, meals, seasons, household chores, taking care of animals, and so forth
- Quality of communication in the family: yelling, avoidance of confrontation, argument, and negative criticism; laughter, humor, and unconditional validation; open-door attitude on all subjects, family respect, and weekly pow-wow to talk about the weeks past and to come; making decisions together, listening to each other
- Discipline: how it was handled, set boundaries, corporal punishment, conversations, who set the family rules, consistent or sporadic follow-through, no consistent consequences, scapegoating, passing the buck or blame
- Style of parenting: creative, authoritative, reliable/ unreliable, secure/insecure, passive/authoritarian, and so forth

How Were You Parented? Who Were Your Role Models?

- Who was the biggest influence in your life?
- Who raised you? What do you remember about how they parented?
- What do you do as a parent or a teacher that comes from your own childhood experience?
- What positive and negative things do you do which are based on the past?

Lower/Foundation/Will/Inner Senses

These are important foundation senses which tell us about ourselves in our own bodies.[26] When they have developed in a healthy manner and are well integrated, we feel secure, safe and centered. When they are not healthy, we can feel anxious, insecure, unsure, unsafe, fearful, on high alert and defensive.

• **Movement** – A proprioceptive experience, this is the sense of our own movement, the ability to coordinate large and fine movements in a purposeful way.

• **Balance** – Vestibular, this is a sense of balance, of safety—can we be secure in our bodies in relationship to gravity and levity?—and gives us the foundation for the ability to be centered in our own selves.

• **Touch** – The tactile sense give us the experience that we end at our skin, that there are boundaries. When children do not have a healthy sense of touch, they do not know where they end and the world begins. Consequently, these children become hyper-vigilant and defensive, feeling that the world is attacking them through their senses, creating anxiety and even aggressive behavior patterns.

• **Life or Well-Being** – Also visceral, this deep sense is directly affected by all of the other eleven senses. When our sense of well-being is compromised, our whole body and being can become overwhelmed and may even shut down. Lack of food, sleep deprivation, motion sickness, physical or verbal threat, test anxiety and many other stressful experiences can negatively impact this primal sense of well-being.

Childhood

The period from birth to age seven is a significant time of physical, sensory, brain and skill development, a time of learning through the will, through action and play. Development proceeds through inhibiting immature movement patterns or automatic reflexes and through a stage of learning by imitation of moral gesture to acquisition of independent skills and the abilities to generalize learned skills independently of the parent or teacher. Dependence turns into a growing age-appropriate independence.

Helping Our Children to Become Independent Individuals

Age-appropriate expectations for our children at each age and stage of development are important. How high or low is the bar set for achievement? If the standards are set for perfection, children become stressed trying to achieve them, or they fall in on themselves because they know it is not possible to reach them. Setting the bar too low and then enabling them tends to dumb children down, also causing a variety of behavioral issues and low self-esteem.

Give them the right kind of assistance, setting the stage for learning and success, by helping them learn how to help themselves. Children are very resourceful and creative when a problem or task is set before them. Allow them opportunity to get on with figuring things out. Otherwise, children grow up being low- or non-achievers and expect others to do for them what they should be doing for themselves. Children can turn off learning by fifth grade if they are not challenged to be engaged in the learning process.

Build self-esteem through experience and not through words alone. Children need to inwardly experience success. Self-esteem is an inner reality and not something pasted onto the outside. When a young child is allowed to explore standing, climbing, walking, one can see the sense of monumental achievement reflected in his/her whole being. Once one task is mastered, the child moves on to the next in the process of becoming. Given the right circumstances, children will challenge themselves. Praise and rewards should be truthful.

Reduce stress by not pushing children to achieve and by reducing chaos at home so that children do not have to carry emotional worries that are not theirs to sort out. Often we see children struggling with issues that are not theirs to start with and for which they do not have the ability to cope. Sometimes children will strike out at the parent with anger, and the parent does not realize that this is merely the child's way of trying to "give back" the issues to the rightful owner.

The consequence of talking to our young children as if they were adults is pressing intellectual, abstract thinking at too early an age, which forces the child to step out of imaginative thinking, rich with meaning, magic and color, into a linear, cold critical world that is foreign to them. Intellectual thinking will rob them of their childhood, thrusting them prematurely into adolescence. What is appropriate for adolescents is not appropriate for young children. They are not ready for the mind games of teens and adults. Engaging them in adult communication only hurts the child in the long run.

Expecting children to understand things from our point of view rather than from their perspective can likewise cause problems. Children think in pictures which are full of meaning. Adults think more intellectually and abstractly. How arrogant is our expectation that children think the way we do, will understand our meaning and thoughts and can communicate with us as adults. How arrogant! Children are full of natural wisdom. When we take the time to understand how they think and operate, we will learn much!

A first grade student was happily drawing a picture when the teacher came over to see what she was doing. "What are you drawing?" asked the teacher.
The child looked up and said, "I am drawing a picture of God," and went on drawing.
The teacher said, "But no one knows what God looks like."
Without skipping a beat the child replied, "But they will in a minute."

DAILY LIFE: RHYTHM, ROUTINE AND RITUAL

Wash on Monday,
Iron on Tuesday,
Mend on Wednesday,
Churn on Thursday,
Clean on Friday,
Bake on Saturday,
Rest on Sunday.
　　　　—traditional English children's verse

The three Rs of daily life—rhythm, routine and ritual—give us a healthy sense and foundation of belonging, security and constancy. Some of our earliest, positive memories center on our childhood experiences of the security and harmony that come from daily rhythms. The morning routine—waking, washing up, eating breakfast, getting off to school—has a huge impact on how a child responds to the day. Walking into a healthy household gives one a feeling of harmony, a lack of chaos. Everything has its place and things are tidy, without the feeling of restriction or "don't touch." Ask a young child in the Waldorf kindergarten what day it is and she will say, "Today is bread baking day" or "Today is stone soup day." The child knows what special activity happens on the particular day of the week. The children feel/know where they belong; what is going to happen next gives them a sense of security and confidence.

Young children do not need endless stimulation and distractions. They can be quite creative given the time and space during the day to just play. At the age of three my niece could spend hours with the pan lids in the drawer under the stove. It was high and secure enough for her to stand holding on with one hand while pulling pan lids out with the other. She also liked to play with the plastic containers and lids in a bottom cupboard while her mother made dinner. Young children need to be near the parent, so parents need to have things to interest children near them as they work and to eventually encourage the children to join in the activity.

Mealtimes are also an important aspect to the rhythm of the day and need to be well planned and prepared by parents. Everyone sits down at the table, which has been set with some care, often by the children through imitating the parent, so that it is pleasing to the eye. Sharing meals offers parents opportunities to discuss the day with the children, to practice listening to each other and to develop conversational and social skills. The mood at meal times also helps train children in healthy habits and attitude towards food and eating. We are in a world culture (especially in the United States) where so many families do not eat together; children and adults rush through meals to get on to something else, often not even chewing their food properly, adding stress to the process of digestion.

What is a household like without the rhythm, routine or daily ritual? Many children, across the whole economic base, arrive at school without breakfast, not wearing appropriate clothes for the weather or the activities of the day, and having skipped personal care altogether. Without rhythm and routine with regards to these daily tasks, the children are unable to integrate into the school environment and are not ready to learn. We are trying to teach children how to one day manage taking care of themselves independently, and so many habits we carry though life comes from early childhood. Over the years the world has speeded up and become so filled with activities, demands and chaos that people feel they have no time for setting slower-paced lives or routines, to a great detriment to us and to our children. No wonder there are more children with nervous, health and behavior disorders. Adults have them too, but we are more able to compensate, hiding or excusing our shortcomings or blaming something or someone else for our lack of will.

> *Before the flour, the mill,*
> *Before the mill, the grain,*
> *Before the grain, the sun and rain,*
> *The beauty of God's will.*

Without rhythm and routine, disorder and chaos fill the void. Many families with well-educated, talented creative adults are so process-oriented that daily routine gets lost. The kitchen is a mess, the house is in perpetual turmoil, and there is a constant feeling of not knowing what matters and no one can find anything. Priorities! This is a hard one to figure out! They are ever-changing, depending on the next crisis in the family. This is a high-energy household; it is unpredictable. Or better said, predictably unpredictable! Something is always happening and there is always room for one more, or five more, at the table. An open door policy is the gesture.

But something happens to the children and to the mother who lives like this; it takes its toll. Children in this environment become either lazy with a "whatever" attitude or they create chaos, quarrel, and are demanding to get what they need and the attention they deserve. What happens to the mother? She might become a screamer; she feels overwhelmed by the demands of her life and family. Her children learn at an early age to turn off their hearing to the volume, intensity and message. To control their environment children will often become either like the parent or overcompensate by keeping his or her room as neat as a pin and the door closed. Many children become responsible, reliable adults despite (to spite!) how they were raised! This is the "reverse" method of learning from the past, turning a negative into the positive by striving to become *not* like the parent. It takes a great deal more energy to achieve, but it is very effective in the long run.

Another important area to be considered is the bedtime routine and ritual. How a person, especially a child, goes to bed at night has a direct impact upon the quality of sleep and how he or she meets the following morning and day.

A mother once told me that her youngest daughter had a terrible time getting up in the morning. She did not want to go to school, did not want to wear the clothes her mother offered, did not like the breakfast—everything was terrible and made her irritable and tearful. I already knew that there was no consistent evening ritual or routine at bedtime and that the child went to bed unhappy. There was a lack of sincere nurturing. The mother, a socially active person, was too involved with her own agenda involving many people and projects outside the family to take genuine interest in her daughter. The child knew this, which fact alone made her feel unwanted and abandoned, especially at night.

The suggestion was made to review the bedtime routine from dinner through "lights-out" at bedtime. There was so much chaos, arguing, negotiating, and stress in the evenings that the child did not go into sleep a "happy camper." As soon as this routine was focused on and a rhythm was established, the child began to wake up happier in the morning.

Whose job is it to establish these routines? Someone needs to take the responsibility—the care-giving parent or grandparent or older child in the family—for this important transition ritual leading from the day in the outer world into the family, then into blessed, renewing sleep. Without this important process children and adults become anxious, irritable, frustrated, depressed and even angry.

- Daily routine and rhythm at home and school help establish healthy boundaries for children. This is especially true for young children who feel safe and secure when their daily routine is predictable and constant.
- Repetition of activities creates security and a sense of foundation for daily life for the child and also for the entire family. Knowing when something is going to happen helps reduce stress and anxiety and allows the soul to be prepared.
- Routine and rhythm provide for the child to experience the age-appropriate activities independently, giving the child the opportunity to be successful through action, to fail and to try again.
- This repetition helps build courage in the child to face the hard tasks with enthusiasm.

- The child needs to be weaned from nursing by nine months and appropriate solid food introduced earlier than six months, depending on child. The child should be weaned from a family bed by three years old, when the independent etheric body begins to emerge.

Boundaries are established for the child's sake. When we delay setting routines that lead to healthy independence in later childhood, it can become very difficult to establish them later, leading to tantrums and oppositional behavior.

It is never too early to learn the basic lessons of daily life. As we get older and, hopefully, wiser, we often forget the simple rules of daily life and tend to make things too complicated. This causes us to miss the priorities and the simple things that have been good and wholesome throughout the ages. A good reminder comes from Robert Fulghum's list of *All I Really Need to Know I Learned in Kindergarten*. Reading them make us smile.

The Golden Rules of Life [27]
1. Share everything.
2. Do not hit people.
3. Put things back where you found them.
4. Clean up your own mess.
5. Do not take things that are not yours.
6. Say you are sorry when you hurt somebody.
7. Wash your hands before you eat.
8. Flush!
9. Warm cookies and cold milk are good for you.
10. Learn some and think some and paint and sing and dance and play and work every day some. Live a balanced life.
11. Take a nap every afternoon.
12. When you go out into the world, watch out for traffic, hold hands and stick together.
13. Be aware of wonder. Remember the little seed in the paper cup: The roots go down and the plant goes up, and nobody really knows how or why, but we are all like that.

14. Goldfish, hamsters and white mice—and even the little seed in the paper cup—they all die. So do we.

15. And then remember Dick and Jane books and the first word you learned—the biggest word of all: "look."

SEASONAL FESTIVALS

Festivals of the seasons and religious holidays are wonderful ways to celebrate deeply-rooted traditions and rituals from early childhood into adulthood. In most families they began many generations ago, reaching into the distant past, giving a sense of belonging and a rightness to the rhythms of life. This can be as simple as the special meals that the family prepares and eats at particular times of the year. When suggesting that a new routine be adopted at a particular time of year, children will rebel and say, "But we always do it that way, and why do we have to change it now?"

Traditions and rituals imprint deeply into the will. We may forget why we are doing something, but we do not forget the feeling of the rightness of the action because it lives deeply in our will. Festivals bring together family, friends, loved ones and even whole communities. This is especially important now when we are so fragmented. There was a time, not so long ago, when we knew everyone in the neighborhood. Everyone felt safe and looked out for each other, celebrating births, marriages and even death. Now we often do not even know our neighbors or our own families.

When they were four and seven years old respectively, my niece and nephew went to see a christening in the Christian Community Church The next morning I woke up hearing a bell ringing downstairs, the exact way it had been rung in the christening service the day before. My sister and I crept down the stairs and peeked over the banister to see what was going on. In the living room below we saw a little altar set up with tiny dishes of water, ashes and sea

99

salt. Spread on the floor in rows were neatly folded towels and upon each little "pew" were dolls and stuffed animals of all shapes and sizes wearing their best dress-up clothes. My niece and nephew were dressed in their mother's and my white half-slips with white blouses over them like the priest and the serving person. My nephew rang the bell and then my niece baptized each doll and stuffed animal that her brother brought forward! It was a solemn occasion performed with deep seriousness and purpose. When it was over my sister and I set a festival table for the children and their newly baptized dollies. We enjoyed a wonderful breakfast party to celebrate and honor the event. The children had a joyous glow and deep calm in them after this experience, especially after it had been acknowledged by the adults while maintaining the mood the children had set in motion.

Often it is the seasonal, religious, spiritual and family rituals that we wish to repeat with our own children later in life. For many families these are the only times when everyone gets together and shares something meaningful. For some families it is the seasonal vacation that is remembered. Or perhaps the Sunday midday meal or other shared activities. These memories become imprinted in us and remain until we take our final breath. Let us strive to make them good and meaningful memories and not ones that our children will have to overcome or try to forget!

Through the festivals and thoughtful customs of life we are able to teach our children respect and reverence for nature, for others and for themselves. The experience of reverence builds a deep wellspring of strength and security in the soul of the child. It will become the source of a healthy moral sense later in life. Children also develop a sense of beauty and truth through the festivals and the care adults take in creating beautiful surroundings for them. These experiences are often lost today because they take time and conscious attention. How many families do not even sit down for dinner together? Or worse, how many have television or other distractions during dinner or, even worse, all day long! How can we ever instill reverence in children in an environment which is designed to do the very opposite, where nothing really matters? It takes conscious work on the part of the parents. In the Waldorf (Steiner) schools reverence, truth and beauty are living principles that are woven into the curriculum and the festivals throughout the year for the creative and healthy effects they have upon the children.

Many wonderful books have been written on how to celebrate seasonal festivals with suggestions for creating celebrations with your children. Young children thrive on repetition and consistency. Setting traditions in the family that will follow your child through life is a very important task. These are times for the family to reconnect after the week of work and school is over. How many families spend all of Saturday riding around in the car for errands, sports events, gymnastics or dance classes? With such a full schedule there is no time to bond and connect. Something "more important" takes the place of genuine family interaction. Then Sunday arrives and everyone is too tired to relate. Yet doing something special and regularly together helps to build a healthy family dynamic and history.

My mom always made animal pancakes on Saturday morning and the neighborhood kids would show up at the back door wanting to join us. There was always room for one more. Daddy was in charge of Sunday breakfast. He would make a big sit-down breakfast and everyone was expected to be there. The rest of the week we were on our own for cold cereal and toast. We got ourselves off to school and would yell up to the second floor for our parents to throw down our lunch money for school. The coins would often fall down into the heating grate and we would have to scramble to fish them out before the bus came. Finally we learned to throw our jackets over the grate. I still don't know why they didn't give us the money the night before.

Traditions are events that we look forward to, like going to summer camp or eating a special dinner on a birthday or at festival times. Traditional meals and dishes at festivals mark the passing of time through the generations. This is especially true in today's world of fast-food, fast-paced, not-enough-time lives, in which we have been brainwashed into believing we need more and more things, to be the consummate consumer even when we do not have the money. Just put it on credit! Well, this does not work with children; it makes them anxious, nervous, fearful and depressed. It undermines their very sense of self, security and trust in themselves and the world. The traditions that are filled with real smells, tastes, colors, words, song and people who love us can heal these wounds of our times. These good memories will grow throughout their entire lives and will continue to be passed down through the generations.[28]

Rhythm of Sleeping and Waking

Why do some children experience difficulty getting a good night's sleep? Why is it so difficult for them to fall asleep, and others struggle to wake up in the morning? What can we do to help these children?

We are living in a world of sense impressions which are often not self-created or self-regulated. It is challenging even for adults to evaluate and digest the many incidental impressions experienced in daily life, without adding various media impressions. For our children this task is sometimes impossible. The stress levels are so high in most of our lives that there hardly seems time to breathe! Yes, the operative word is *breathe*. We do not simply breathe with our lungs, but with our whole body and being. The gesture of today is one of inhalation, a gesture of fear, and it is becoming more and more difficult to truly exhale. Our whole rhythmic system is off balance and needs harmonizing. This has a direct impact on sleeping and waking.

Children who have difficulty falling asleep often suffer from too many sense impressions which they cannot fully digest (integrate into a meaningful context). At the same time they cannot let go of them. We experience this as adults when we lie awake in the middle of the night still thinking of work or some event that has happened or will happen the next day. Children experience many unvoiced fears and anxieties that to an adult seem manageable, unimportant or trivial, but to the child are overwhelming, intense, and real. How can we help our children establish a healthy rhythm of sleeping and waking?

Children who have a fear of falling asleep need reassurance that their parents will be there in the morning (especially mom) and

103

that all will be well. These children need to trust and feel secure. They can be helped by previewing at night the activities of the next morning—getting ready for school: what they will wear and the breakfast they will eat; their teacher who will be waiting for them at school; and the first lesson of the day. It is vital that the parent then follow through on what was said and be on time picking up the child from school or be home when he/she gets there. A nutritional or calming lavender bath at night can also be helpful. A set routine at bedtime with an evening ritual, candle, a story and a bedtime verse is very reassuring.

Children who cannot let go of the day need help in sorting out their feelings. Talking through what has taken place during the day and about their worries is one way. Reducing and monitoring what type of impressions the child receives, especially before bed at night, is very important (no television, video games, homework right before bed). Deep pressure massage of the lower legs and feet can calm the nervous activity of the head. For some children a light snack before bedtime helps them sleep through the night.

Children who cannot wake in the morning go so deeply into sleep that it is actually painful for them to wake in the morning. Be ready before your child is up. Have all clothes laid out the night before to reduce morning decisions. Wake them with a warm washcloth with a bit of lemon or rosemary essence to help them wake up while they are still in bed. Get a warm drink in them (warm honey tea) before they reach the breakfast table. Everything should be packed and ready to go for school the night before so that there is no searching at the last minute. Have the child make and pack the lunch the night before. Do not forget the jacket—warmth is so important in this whole picture.

For parent and child survival, the key to morning routines is being ahead of the pack! The morning parent, usually the mom, is well-advised to be up and able at least one half hour before the children get up, and ready to focus on the needs of the children. The morning will be less chaotic, children will be happier and parents will feel better able to cope and feel successful. Everyone has a greater chance to have a good day!

Anyone who does not get a good night's sleep is ill-disposed. Lack of sleep has a direct impact upon our sense of well-being and health. When this foundation sense is not in balance, children and adults alike are not able to function properly. Many children come to school without breakfast, cranky and sleepy, not dressed warmly enough, and having forgotten half their things for school. What kind of day would you have at work if you started your day like this?

Children need a good breakfast before they come to school to be ready and able to learn. Often children today begin the morning on an empty stomach, no breakfast at all, causing them to be restless or listless, unfocused and cranky. This creates many obstacles to learning and in social interactions. Plan ahead, even prepare or lay out breakfast the night before.

Choose your battles wisely. Determine what the real issues are and deal with them appropriately. Children cannot put themselves to bed at night; a parent is required. The quality of the bedtime ritual will set the tone for the morning. If there is chaos at night, there will be chaos in the morning.

- Children who tend to wake in the night and crawl in with the parents or who cannot fall asleep without a parent lying beside them are children who tend to need more deep pressure touch to feel secure in their bodies.
- Children who are bed-wetters sleep deeply and do not rouse when they need to urinate. These children can be helped with therapeutic eurythmy addressed specifically to the kidney organization.
- Nightmares are often organically based or stem from emotional stress in the child's surroundings.
- Sleepwalking indicates that the forces of the moon are working deeply upon the child and need to be addressed through remedies and therapeutic eurythmy.

There are exercises described in *The Extra Lesson* to assist children with sleeping and waking. These exercises help to harmonize the relationship between the astral and etheric bodies, thus promoting a more rhythmic breathing of the soul.

Reflections and Conclusion

The principal challenge of parenting is the day-to-day reality. We can train to be a good teacher through study and we can create fantastic and clever lessons for our students, but the proof of our effectiveness as a teacher lies in who we are, not in our showmanship. Who we really are, our authentic self, is revealed when we stand in front of the children and begin to teach. Not our knowledge alone, but who we are, teaches the children.

This is also true for parents. Who one is guides, nurtures and educates the children. That is why it is so important to be always changing oneself, learning, growing, adapting. Over the temple thresholds in ancient Greece were the words, "Man: know thyself." Everything comes back to us. Once we reach adulthood, we must begin to take responsibility for our own actions or inactions, our intentions and how they impact those around us.

Even with the wealth of information available to parents today, it still comes down to the daily routine, relationship and progress of life. How do we meet each event presented to us by our children? How can we truly prepare ourselves to be awake and balanced in meeting their needs and educating them into life's wonder and challenge? How can we teach children to be healthy, honest individuals who have the courage to do their best, even when life is challenging? As I say to my students, "It is not that you fall down or fail. The important thing is that you have the courage to get up, learn from your mistakes and try again." By and large, we adults have promoted a false self-esteem in today's children and have enabled them in such away that they do not always or often try their best. Or we expect such a high level of perfection from them that they give up when they are not "perfect." We have put children of all ages between a rock and a hard place. They need our help to get free of this entrapment.

We are living in a time which is challenging every day. Inundated as we are with an avalanche of information that can be overwhelming to sort out and understand, we will find the answers to our questions when we take the time to quiet ourselves and go inward. Almost all the parents I have met know their children, whether they realize it or not. But they have not learned to trust their instincts and their bond with their children whom they allow then to disempower them and exacerbate the problem. But when parents are helped to listen to their children, to perceive their children as they really are, then a feeling of empowerment and love arises in their souls and healing can begin.

Everything worth having or achieving takes introspection and work. The results of our deeds are astoundingly rewarding and are directly visible in our children. Our choices about how we raise our children will come to fruition as they become adults. It is said that children are our future. Each child is a unique and precious part of the universe, and how we parent, guide, educate and nurture them will determine how they will be as adults. What we are doing each day impacts the future for all of us.

ENDNOTES

1. Antoine de Saint Exupéry, *The Little Prince*, New York and London: Harcourt Brace Jovanovich, 1971, pp. 93.

2. Nancy Darling, PhD, *Parenting Style and Its Correlates, Clearinghouse on Elementary and Early Childhood Education*, EDO-PS-99-3, March 1999. From Maccoby, E.E. & J.A. Martin. "Socialization in the Context of the Family: Parent–Child Interaction." In P.H. Mussen (ed.) & E.M. Hetherington (vol. ed.), *Handbook of Child Psychology: Vol. 4. Socialization, personality, and social development* (4th ed., pp. 1–101), New York: Wiley, 1983.

3. Rudolf Steiner, *The Four Temperaments*, New York: Anthroposophic Press, 1968, p. 22.

4. Ibid., p. 12.

5. Knud Asbjorn Lund, *Understanding Our Fellow Human Beings,* East Grinstead, UK: New Knowledge Books, 1965, pp. 62-63.

6. Rudolf Steiner, *Prayers for Mothers and Children*, London: Rudolf Steiner Press, 1983, p. 27.

7. Arthur L. Hayward, *Cassell's Compact English Dictionary*, London: Cassell & Co., 1968.

8. John D. Eliot, PhD, *Reverse Psychology for Success, The Quotations Page*, www.quotationspage.com.

9. This is an expansion by the author (May 2006) of descriptions provided by K.H. Grobman in a website article "Theory of Parenting Styles: Original Description of the Styles," based on material originally published by Diana Baumrind in an article titled "Child Care Practices Anteceding Three Patterns of Preschool Behavior," *Genetic Psychology Monographs*, 75(1), 1967, pp. 43–88.

10. Susan Forward, PhD, *Toxic Parents: Overcoming Their Hurtful Legacy and Reclaiming Your Life*, New York: Bantam Dell Publishing Group, January 2002, pp. 5–6.

11. Johann Wolfgang von Goethe, *Faust*, Translated by John Anster, 1935, lines 214–230, www.artquotations.com.

12. Rudolf Steiner, *Knowledge of Higher Worlds*, New York: Anthroposophic Press, 1961, pp. 33–35.

13. Attributed to Johann Wolfgang von Goethe (Faust), referenced by: William Hutchinson Murray (1913–1996), in *The Scottish Himalayan Expedition*, London: Dent, 1951.

14. Rudolf Steiner, *Curative Education*, a series of 12 lectures given in 1924, London: Rudolf Steiner Press, 1998, pp. 39–40.

15. Ibid., p. 31.

16. Ibid., p. 41.

17. Rudolf Steiner, *Education for Special Needs, The Curative Education Course*, Lecture 2, London: Rudolf Steiner Press, 1998, pp. 39–40.

18. Ibid., p. 40.

19. Excerpted from *Investigation and Prosecution of Child Abuse*, 3rd Edition, authored by the American Prosecutors Research Institute, National Center for Prosecution of Child Abuse, Alexandria, VA, Thousand Oaks, CA: Sage Publications, 2003.

20. L. Alan Sroufe, Robert Cooper and Ganie DeHart, *Child Development, Its Nature and Course*, New York: McGraw-Hill, Inc., 1992, pp. 200–217.

21. Leonard Cohen, "Anthem," from *The Essential Leonard Cohen*, album *The Future*.

22. Kahlil Gibran, "Parents," *The Prophet*, New York: Alfred A Knopf, Inc. Random House, 1923, p. 15.

23. Audrey McAllen, *The Extra Lesson*, Fair Oaks, CA: Rudolf Steiner College Press, 2004.

24. Hennig Köhler, translated by Marjorie Spock, *Working with Anxious, Nervous, and Depressed Children, A Spiritual Perspective to Guide Parents*, Fair Oaks, CA: AWSNA Publications, 2001.

25. Phillip McGraw, MD, *Family First: Your Step-by-Step Plan for Creating a Phenomenal Family*, New York: Simon & Schuster, 2004.

26. Material for this section can be referenced in: Rudolf Steiner, *A Psychology of Body, Soul, and Spirit*, Anthroposophic Press, 1999; and Albert Soesman, *Our Twelve Senses*, Stroud, UK: Hawthorn Press, 1990.

27. Robert Fulghum, *All I Really Need to Know I Learned in Kindergarten*, New York: Fawcett Columbine, 1988, pp. 6–7.

28. Gudrun Davy & Bons Voors, *Lifeways: Working with Family Questions, A Parent's Anthology*, Stroud, UK: Hawthorn Press, 1983, pp. 36–39.

BIBLIOGRAPHY

Baldwin-Dancy, Rahima. *You Are Your Child's First Teacher*, Berkeley, CA: Celestial Arts, 2000.

Darling, Nancy. *Parenting Style and Its Correlates,Clearinghouse on Elementary and Early Childhood Education*, EDO-PS-99-3, March 1999. From Maccoby, E.E. & J.A. Martin. "Socialization in the Context of the Family: Parent–Child Interaction." In P.H. Mussen (ed.) & E.M. Hetherington (vol. ed.), *Handbook of Child Psychology: Vol. 4*. Socialization, personality, and social development (4th ed.), New York: Wiley, 1983.

Davy, Gudrun and Bon Voors. *Lifeways: Working with Family Questions*, Stroud, UK: Hawthorn Press, 1983.

de Saint Exupéry, Antoine. *The Little Prince*, New York and London: Harcourt Brace Jovanovich, 1971.

Fulghum, Robert. *All I Really Needed to Know I Learned in Kindergarten*, New York: Fawcett Columbine, 1988.

Goddard-Blythe, Sally. *The Well-Balanced Child, Movement and Early Learning*, Stroud, UK: Hawthorn Press, 2004.

Goldhor, Lerner, H. *The Dance of Anger,* New York: Harper & Row Publishers, 1985.

Holtzapfel, W. *Children's Destinies*, Spring Valley, NY: Mercury Press, 1984.

Köhler, Hennig. *Working with Anxious, Nervous and Depressed Children*, Fair Oaks, CA: AWSNA Publications, 2001.

König, Karl. *The First Three Years of the Child*, New York: Anthroposophic Press, 1969.

_____. *Brothers and Sisters, a Study in Child Psychology*, New York: Steiner Books, 1991.

McAllen, Audrey. *The Extra Lesson*, Fair Oaks, CA: Rudolf Steiner College Press, 2004.

McGraw, Phillip. *Family First: Your Step-by-Step Plan for Creating a Phenomenal Family*, New York: Simon & Schuster, 2004.

Peck, M. Scott. *People of the Lie*, New York: Simon & Schuster, 1983.

Steiner, Rudolf. *Education for Special Needs: The Curative Education Course* (Dornach, June 25–July 7, 1924), London: Rudolf Steiner Press, 1998.

_____. *Prayers for Mothers & Children* (Dornach, February 2, 1915), London: Rudolf Steiner Press, 1983.

_____. *A Psychology of Body, Soul and Spirit* (12 lectures, October 23–27, 1909–1910 and December 12–16, 1911), New York: SteinerBooks, 1999.

_____. *Reincarnation and Karma, How Karma Works* [also under new publication title *Reincarnation and Karma: Two Fundamental Truths of Human Existence* (5 lectures, Berlin and Stuttgart, January–March 1912), New York: SteinerBooks, 1962.